UNDERSTANDING

WHAT MANAGERS NEED TO KNOW

Second Edition

By: Mary L. Lo Re, PhD

Printed in the United States of America
ISBN 978-1-7329858-0-3

PREFACE

INTENDED AUDIENCE

This book is intended for readers who are interested in understanding how the various fields of economics play a role in their everyday personal and/or professional lives.

Having had extensive business and academic careers, I conducted lengthy research to find appropriate course material for the Managerial Economics course. What I came to realize was the importance and need for a book that presented a micro, macro, and international perspective that would enable students not only to understand the theories and assumptions of economics but also to realize the forces that push consumers, producers, and governments to make economic decisions. Furthermore, the material would encourage readers to truly relate these perspectives to their own lives so that they could ultimately make informed and effective economic choices.

Keeping these objectives in mind, I was inspired to write such a book using real-world national and international examples, simple language, and basic calculations, while presenting wide-ranging economic concepts.

This text is typically best used in programs in which students are only exposed to one course in (or a comprehensive view of) economics. Alternatively, it can be used as a primer for further in-depth courses or programs of study in business or economics.

Organization of the Text

This book is organized into three sections and concludes with a Works Cited and an Index for ready referencing.

Section One is a basic introduction to the field of economics, its subfields, basic definitions and assumptions in the field. Section Two begins with an understanding of microeconomics. Highlights from this section include discussions of demand, supply, and equilibrium; classification of goods; slope; elasticity; market disruptions; and business structures (including game theory) and their effect on market equilibrium. Section Three begins with an understanding of macroeconomics. Highlights from this section include discussions of the concept of GDP and all components of its expenditure approach; economic growth; foreign exchange and risk management; unemployment; inflation; economic indicators; money and banking; and monetary and fiscal policy.

In all these chapters, current statistical data is presented to support the theories. Relevant real-world domestic and international examples, as well as graphics, and case-scenarios, are also used to further explain concepts. Moreover, where math is used, step-by-step calculations are shown to arrive at each solution. Lastly, each chapter concludes with five "Testing Your Knowledge" questions or statements.

Instructor Resources

PowerPoint slides accompanying this book, answers and explanations for the "Testing Your Knowledge" questions at the end of each chapter, and sample exam questions may be requested through Sentia Publishing and/or by contacting the author directly. Please feel free to also contact the author with any questions or suggestions for expanding the material presented in this book. The author may be contacted via email at mlore@wagner.edu.

ACKNOWLEDGEMENTS

I would like to thank my students, colleagues, and friends—especially those that have contributed to this body of work (see citations within)—and above all, my family, who have supported me in following my passion to become an educator and my continuous search to seek and share knowledge. A deep and heartfelt gratitude to all!

ABOUT THE AUTHOR:

Dr. Mary L. Lo Re is a professor of finance and the director of experiential learning and internships at the Wagner College Nicolais School of Business. Previously, Dr. Lo Re held the following leadership positions at that institution: dean of adult education and extension programs, interim associate provost, chair of the Department of Business Administration, director of MBA programs, and director of assessment.

Dr. Lo Re obtained her PhD from the Graduate Center of the City University of New York specializing in monetary theories/policies and international trade. She has written and obtained many external and internal grants; and her work with her students and the community has received numerous multi-media mentions. Additionally, she has presented and published many peer-reviewed journal articles on EU/EMU economic growth, convergence, exchange rates, and corruption; the economic financial crisis; civic engagement/service-learning; and best practices such as writing across the curriculum.

In addition to this book, Dr. Lo Re is the author of *Experiential Civic Learning: Construction of Models & Assessment.* She has also authored two book chapters: "Service-Learning Community: A Win for Students, Community, Institution & Faculty" in *Service-Learning Pedagogy: How Does It Measure Up?* and, "Balancing Management & Leadership" in *The Resource Handbook for Academic Deans.*

Prior to academia, Dr. Lo Re obtained 17 years of practical business experience—including nine years in computer technology and risk modeling and five years in executive management—working at American Express, the United Nations, and the Board of Education District Office. Her areas of teaching and research include finance, economics, data analysis, and international business.

TABLE OF CONTENTS

PART I. INTRODUCTION TO ECONOMICS

CHAPTER 1.

A MANAGERIAL UNDERSTANDING OF ECONOMICS

Chapter 1. A Managerial Understanding of Economics

Economics is considered a social science which is comprised of many fields and subfields. At its basic level, it is divided into two major fields: microeconomics and macroeconomics. However, the field is vast, and the following classification system will give you a good indication as to its many categories.

Fields in Economics:

The Journal of Economic Literature has developed a classification system—used to classify articles, books, book reviews, dissertations, and working papers—to categorize the fields in economics. The journal cites the economic categories, in alphabetical order, as follows: [1]

- agricultural & natural resource economics-environmental & ecological economics
- business administration & business economics-marketing-accounting-personnel economics
- economic development, innovation, technological change & growth
- economic history
- economic systems
- financial economics
- general economics and teaching
- health, education & welfare
- history of economic thought, methodology & heterodox approaches
- industrial organization

[1] JEL Classification System / EconLit Subject Descriptors, 2017.

- international economics
- labor & demographic economics
- law & economics
- macroeconomics & monetary economics
- mathematical & quantitative methods
- microeconomics
- miscellaneous categories
- other special topics
- public economics
- urban, rural, regional, real estate & transportation economics

In addition, there are other fields within economics that have developed after the creation of the Journal of Economic Literature's classification. Some of these include behavioral economics, market design, organizational economics, political economy, and social choice theory.

Naturally, given one course in managerial economics, we cannot possibly cover all these topics. However, we will highlight a mixture of these economic concepts in this book to help you have a broad understanding of economics and how it can help you make more informed decisions as well as make you a more knowledgeable person and manager.

Economics Defined:

I am sure you have heard the term "economics" and may have also taken a course in economics either in high school or in college. But if this is your first course in economics, or as a refresher, I would first like to focus your attention on the definition of "economics." Economics is the study of how people or managers make decisions given scarce resources.

SCARCE RESOURCES:

So, what are these "scarce resources?" Scarce resources are assets used to produce goods (tangibles, such as wood or iron) or services (intangibles, such as tutoring or chimney cleaning) that are not in abundance.

These scarce resources can be classified into five categories:

1. Natural resources

"Natural resources" refers to land, fertility of the soil, water, minerals, oil, gas, forests, and so forth—all resources that exist without human intervention and are supplied by nature.

2. Labor

"Labor" refers to the physical and mental effort put forth by individuals (or laborers) in productive activities. This may include the number of hours an accountant spends working to reconcile the books, or the number of packages a worker produces in a week.

3. Capital

"Capital" refers to goods made by individuals for usage in productive activities (i.e., that can be used to produce other goods). This includes buildings, machinery, etc.[2]

4. Human capital

"Human capital" refers to the educational, social, and personal skills, talents, and experience of individuals used to perform labor. Human capital is not equal to labor.

---

[2] Please note that while in other fields of study, the term "capital" is used to refer to "money"; in economics, capital $\neq$ money!

5. Entrepreneurship

"Entrepreneurship" is the ability to organize, operate, assume risk, and make decisions—in response to how, how much, what, where, and when—in the running of an enterprise. Entrepreneurship is not equal to human capital.

After specifying what we mean by "scarce resources" and its five categories, let's further define what we mean by "scarce" or "scarcity." Scarcity refers to the fact that the above categories of resources are not in abundance; there is no endless supply of these resources.[3] The concept of scarcity, both from social psychology and economics, stems from the hypothesis that people's wants to satisfy their needs are unlimited—people are never fully satisfied and place a higher value on things that are scarce!

So, are scarcity and shortage the same thing? No. The scenario in figure 1 highlights this difference.

SCARCITY VS. SHORTAGE:

Figure 1. "Scarcity vs. shortage" scenario

WOW! I really like this Maserati—look at this beauty! The Gran Turismo Sport starting price is set at $177,890. There is only one problem...
I do not have this kind of cash!

[3] There exists a finite number of available natural resources; there is only so much labor a worker can put forth as well as the amount of capital a worker can produce in a day. In addition, at any one point in time, individuals have a finite knowledge acquisition base, and not everyone has entrepreneurial abilities.

In the scenario from figure 1, is the lack of funds (i.e., money) an example of a scarcity or a shortage? The answer is shortage! Why? For money to be scarce, it would have to fall under one of the five previously listed scarce resources. Money is not an economic resource and should not be confused to mean "capital." (You may want to revisit the definition of "capital"!) While money can be used to buy materials or pay laborers to create a capital good, the term "money" is not interchangeable with the term "capital" in economics! Therefore, being short on cash is a shortage situation and not a scarcity issue.

Okay, but what if the ending of the scenario in figure 1 was changed to say, "There is only one problem…the manufacturer stated that this car is currently out of stock!" Is this an example of scarcity? The answer again is no. Why? Ask yourself, is the car a capital resource? No, it is not; the car is the final product produced that used the "scarce resources." Therefore, this is an example of a shortage. In sum, scarcity ≠ shortage!

Can you create other scenarios that demonstrate why each of the five scarce resources is indeed "scarce"?

MICRO– *VS.* MACROECONOMICS:

As stated previously, the body of economics can be studied from two major perspectives: micro- and macroeconomics.

Microeconomics is the branch of economics that studies how individuals, households, firms and/or industries (from a one-unit perspective) behave and make choices given unlimited wants and scarce resources. Some topics studied in microeconomics, in no particular order, include market equilibrium, consumer behavior, profit maximization, cost minimization, break-even analysis, business structures, and game theory.

Macroeconomics, on the other hand, is the branch of economics that studies how decisions are made at the national level. Some topics studied in macroeconomics, in no particular order, include inflation, unemployment, the business cycle, gross domestic product, money & banking, monetary & fiscal policy, international trade, and currency exchange.

Managers need to study microeconomics in order to make decisions that will best benefit themselves, their unit, department, and company; however, without an understanding of macroeconomics, they will not be able to fully understand how their unit/department/company's decisions are impacted by elements affecting the economy at large. That is why this book highlights some of the major topics in both major subfields of economics. Moreover, as a result of increased globalization, this book includes a chapter on currency exchange and suggestions for controlling financial and nonfinancial risk.

ASSUMPTIONS IN ECONOMICS:

As you read the following chapters, it would be helpful for you to note that the study of economics makes certain assumptions.

- ***Rational buyers and sellers***

  Both buyers and sellers, based on their rational outlook, available information, and past experiences, make trades that increase their economic utility or satisfaction level and make no trades that do not increase their utility or satisfaction level.

- ***Ceteris paribus***

  Ceteris paribus, Latin for "everything else equal," is applied to any factor, element, or event assuming everything else is held constant (i.e., does not change). As an example, "*Ceteris paribus*, you will complete this course" means that, everything else held constant (or with no unexpected changes), you will complete this course.

- ***More is preferred to less***

  As economic agents or participants (i.e., buyers and sellers that engage in the market in an economic activity) need to make decisions, the field of economics assumes that economic agents can make a choice between two or more options. In making this choice, economic participants prefer having more as opposed to having less.

While you may argue and offer examples where these assumptions do not hold, please bear in mind that these assumptions are drawn primarily from the field of consumer behavior and refer to the economy as a whole, not to any one particular economic participant.[4]

[4] If you are interested in the study of consumer behavior, you may want to read the works of Richard H. Thaler, PhD, University of Chicago who was honored with the 2017 Nobel Prize in Economics for his research in the field of behavioral economics.

TESTING YOUR KNOWLEDGE *(I.E., YOUR ACQUIRED HUMAN CAPITAL)*

Determine whether the following questions are true or false. If false, can you explain why?

1. Is money "capital"?
2. Are the concepts of scarcity and shortage interchangeable?
3. Is entrepreneurship human capital?
4. Is a capital good a natural resource?
5. Does the study of the sneaker industry in the United States fall under the branch of macroeconomics?

PART II. MICROECONOMICS

CHAPTER 2.

THE IMPORTANCE OF DEMAND & SUPPLY

CHAPTER 3.

CLASSIFICATION OF GOODS, SLOPE & ELASTICITY

CHAPTER 4.

NEW EQUILIBRIUM: SHIFTS IN DEMAND & SUPPLY

CHAPTER 5.

MARKET DISRUPTIONS

CHAPTER 6.

BUSINESS STRUCTURES & EFFECT ON MARKET EQUILIBRIUM

CHAPTER 2. THE IMPORTANCE OF DEMAND & SUPPLY

UNDERSTANDING DEMAND:

When we talk about demand, we are referring to individual consumers of goods or services. This is important to remember in understanding the inverse relationship between the quantity demanded of a good/product or service and its price.

Demand, put simply, is what a consumer, individual, household, firm, or industry wants and values. It naturally follows that if you demand a product or service, you place a value or a price on that product or service. However, consumer behavior tells us that, *ceteris paribus*, a consumer prefers to pay a lower price.[5] This is evidenced when stores announce they will slash prices (i.e., hold sales). As examples, during Black Friday, Cyber Monday, January white sales, and other sale days, consumption (i.e., total dollar and amount of purchases by consumers) increases.

LAW OF DEMAND:

Thus, the law of demand states that, on average, the higher the price, the lower the quantity demanded for a product or service. Conversely, the lower the price, the higher the quantity demanded (i.e., wanted) will be for a product or service. There exists an indirect, inverse, or negative relationship between the quantity demanded (Qd) for a product/service and its price (P). Symbolically, we can write "when P ↑, Qd ↓" and "when P ↓, Qd ↑."

[5] *Ceteris paribus,* discussed in Chapter 1, is a Latin term which means "everything else held constant." In this sentence, it refers to the same quality of the product or service.

In order to visually see the law of demand at work, let's see how a demand curve is graphed.

UNDERSTANDING A GRAPH:

A graph is a visual representation of the relationship between two variables. When drawn, each of the axes (lines) represents a different variable. If we assume that we are only interested in seeing a demand curve containing only positive values (that is, with no negative quantities or negative prices), then these two axes will form a right angle (90°) where the two lines intersect at the value of zero. Graphically, this will look like figure 1.

Figure 1. X- and Y-axis graphed

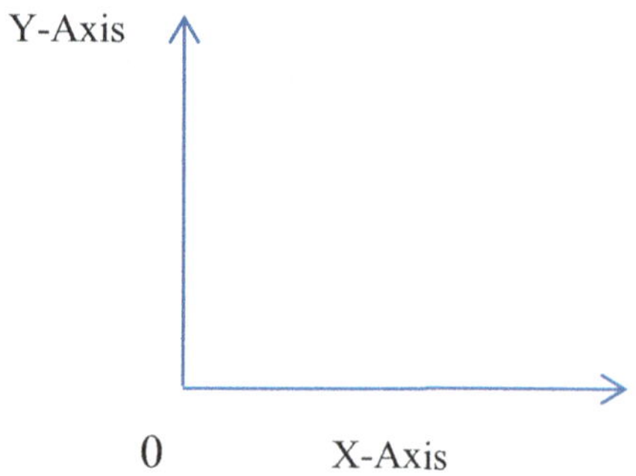

The vertical line in figure 1 is referred to as the "Y-axis" while the horizontal line is referred to as the "X-axis." Each of the axes (timelines) represents a different variable. Conventionally, in graphing the demand curve, we measure the variable price on the Y-axis and the variable quantity demanded on the Y-axis. See figure 2.

Figure 2. Price and quantity demanded graphed

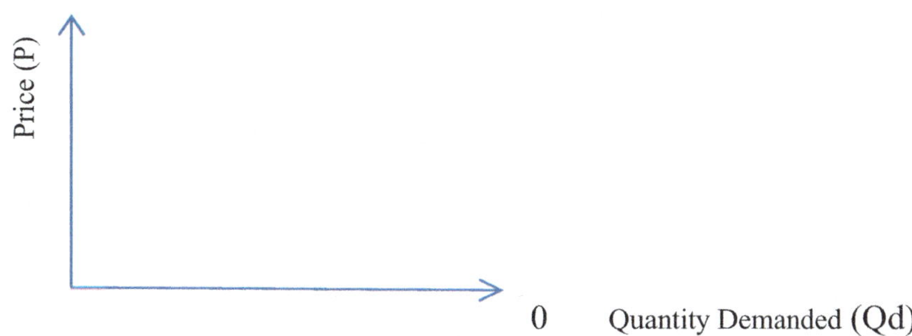

In creating a graph of the demand curve, we first need to know the quantity that is demanded at a particular price. We can do this by establishing a table.

Demand Table/Schedule:

A demand table (i.e., referred to as a demand schedule) provides the quantity demanded of a good at a particular price. As an example, let's say we ask a consumer who likes Twix chocolate bars how many total bars of chocolate s/he would be willing to demand (or consume) during a seven-day week at particular prices. In tabular form, this individual's demand schedule may look something like figure 3.

Figure 3. Demand schedule for Twix chocolate bars (per week)

Price per Bar (P)	**Quantity Demanded** (Qd)
$0.50	70
$0.75	63
$1.00	56
$1.25	49
$1.50	42
$1.75	35
$2.00	28
$2.25	21
$2.50	14
$2.75	7
$3.00	0

We can interpret the demand schedule in figure 3 as follows: at a price of $0.50, 70 Twix chocolate bars will be demanded per week; however, s/he is not willing to purchase any Twix chocolate bars (i.e., Qd = 0) should the price be set at $3.00. In reviewing the combination of price and quantity demanded from the demand schedule, we can see that this exhibits the law of demand in that as price rises, the quantity demanded decreases, and vice versa. Using the P and Qd data from Figure 3, we can plot the demand schedule on a graph.

DEMAND CURVE GRAPHED:

Figure 4 is a graphical representation of the above demand schedule (fig. 3).

Figure 4. Graph of demand schedule for Twix chocolates bars (per week)

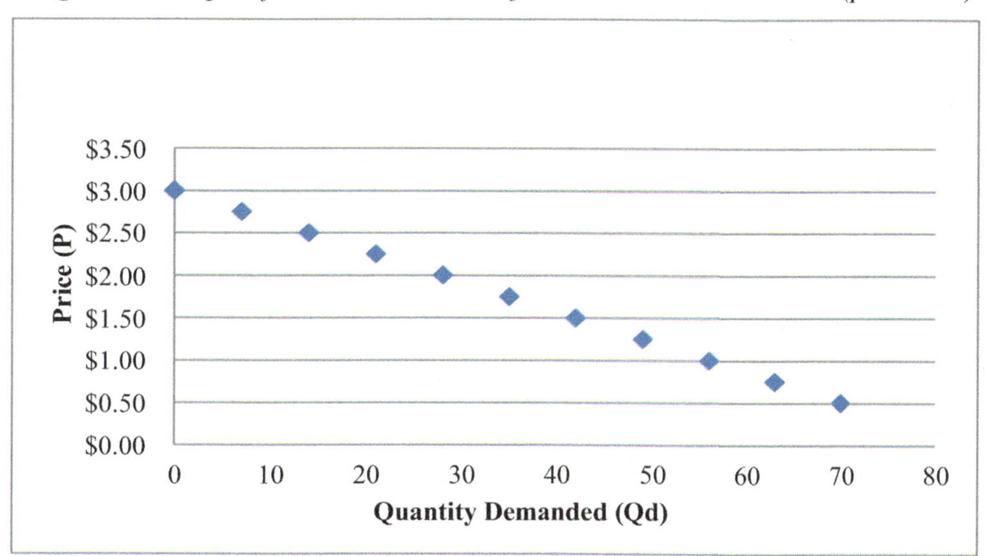

Every dot in figure 4 represents the combination of price and quantity demanded from the table shown in figure 3. The top dot (upper left) represents the last coordinates of Qd (0) and P ($3) from the demand schedule—no chocolate will be demanded at a price of $3 per bar. The bottom dot (lower right) represents the fact that 70 bars of chocolate will be demanded per week when the price per bar is $0.50.

If you now connect the dots in the graph shown in figure 4, you will have what is called a demand curve. The demand curve is downward sloping exhibiting the law of demand. Please notice that in this case, the demand curve is linear (i.e., traveling in a straight line). This is because the incremental changes in both the price and quantity demanded are constant—price changes by twenty-five cents and quantity demanded changes by seven units. However, for another consumer or another product or service, you should know that not all incremental changes in price and quantity demanded will be constant. In these cases (i.e., when the incremental changes in price and corresponding quantity demanded of the product/service are not constant), the demand curve, while still downward sloping, may be nonlinear. A graphical example of a nonlinear demand curve can be seen in figure 5.

Figure 5. Nonlinear demand curve for Twix chocolate bars (per week)

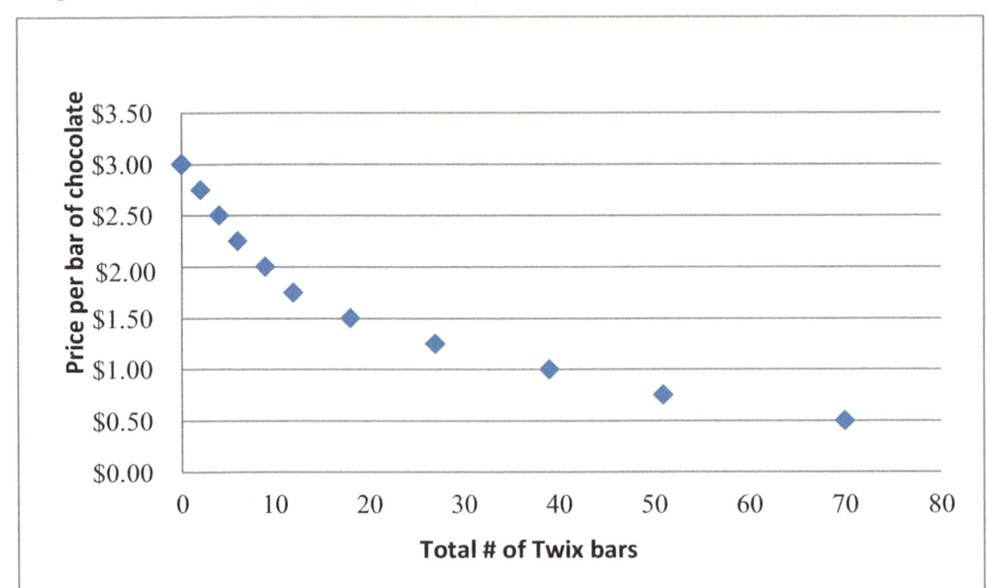

Understanding Supply:

In contrast to demand, where we are referring to consumers, when we talk about supply, we are referring to individuals that produce and/or sell a product or service. This is important to remember in understanding the positive relationship that exists between the quantity supplied of a product or service and its price.

Put simply, supply is what a supplier, manufacturer, firm, or industry is willing to produce (or put forth/carry in his/her store) at a certain price. It naturally follows that if a product or service can command a higher price (i.e., a supplier can charge more for product/service), a supplier will be willing to supply more of that product or service. As an example, if you were a supplier of sneakers and you knew that (1) the average male shoe size in the United States is 10.5[6] and (2) Baller brand sneakers can command a higher sticker price than Jordan sneakers[7], naturally, you would be willing to supply more Baller brand sneakers in size 10.5 than Jordan sneakers. (Can you see how the economic assumptions discussed in Chapter 1 apply to this situation?)

LAW OF SUPPLY:

Thus, the law of supply states that, on average, the higher the price, the higher the quantity supplied. Conversely, the lower the price, the lower the quantity supplied. There exists a direct, or positive (i.e., both variables move in the same direction), relationship between the quantity supplied (Qs) for a product/service and its price (P).

Symbolically, we can write, "when P ↑, Qs ↑" and "when P ↓, Qs ↓."

Before graphically creating a supply curve, we will need to know the quantity of products or services that will be supplied at a particular price. Paralleling the construction of the demand schedule for the previously discussed Twix chocolate bars example, we can establish a table of prices and the corresponding quantity supplied by a given supplier.

---

[6] See Statistic Brain, 2017.

[7] See Chin, 2017.

SUPPLY TABLE/SCHEDULE:

In tabular form, this firm's Twix chocolate bar supply schedule may look something like figure 6.

Figure 6. Supply schedule for Twix chocolate bars (per week)

Price (P)	Quantity Supplied (Qs)
$0.50	0
$0.75	7
$1.00	14
$1.25	21
$1.50	28
$1.75	35
$2.00	42
$2.25	49
$2.50	56
$2.75	63
$3.00	70

From the supply schedule, we can observe that this firm is not willing to supply (or sell) any Twix chocolate bars at a price of $0.50 (i.e., Qs = 0); but at higher prices, the firm is willing to supply/sell more chocolate bars per week. We can also see that this supply schedule exhibits the law of supply in that as price rises, the quantity supplied also rises, and vice versa. We can now plot the supply schedule on a graph. Do you think the supply curve will be downward sloping as in the case of the demand curve?

SUPPLY CURVE GRAPHED:

Figure 7 is a graphical representation of the above supply schedule (fig. 6). Did you guess that the supply curve would be upward sloping?

Figure 7. Graph of supply schedule for Twix chocolate bars (per week)

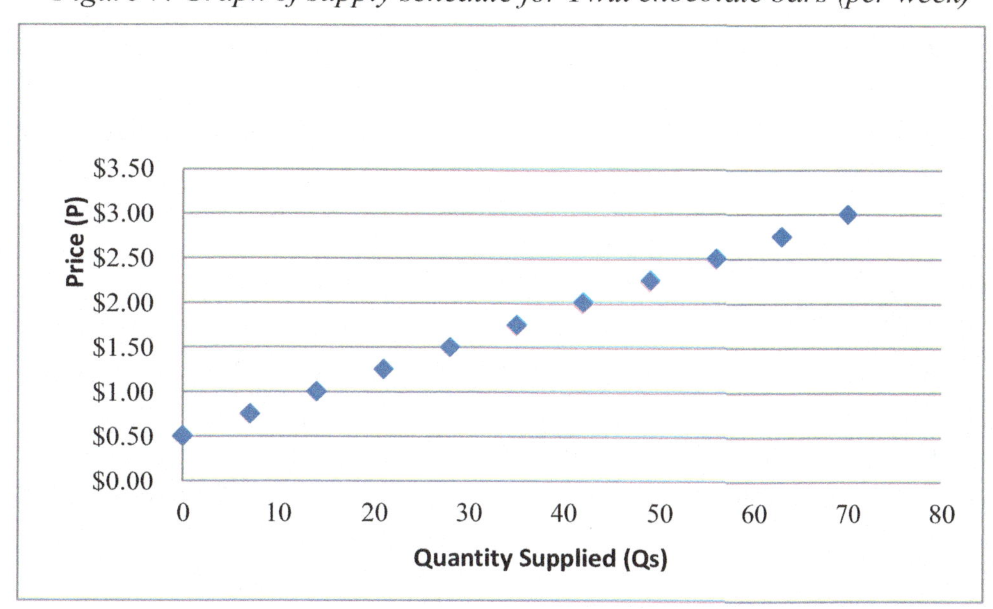

Every dot in figure 7 represents the combination of price and quantity supplied from the table shown in figure 6. The bottom dot (lower left) represents the first coordinates of Qs (0) and P ($0.50) from the supply schedule—no Twix chocolate bars will be supplied at a price of $0.50 per bar. The top dot (upper right) represents the fact that 70 Twix chocolate bars will be supplied per week when the price of each bar is $3.00.

If you now connect the dots in the graph shown in figure 7, you will have what is called a supply curve. The supply curve is upward sloping exhibiting the law of supply. Please notice that in this case, once again, the supply curve is linear (a straight line). This is because the incremental changes in both the price and quantity supplied are constant—price changes by twenty-five cents and quantity supplied changes by seven units. However, not all incremental changes in price and quantity supplied will be constant; thus, for another supplier, the supply curve, while still upward sloping and exhibiting the law of supply, may be nonlinear (as seen in figs. 8*a* and 8*b*).

Figure 8a. Nonlinear supply curve

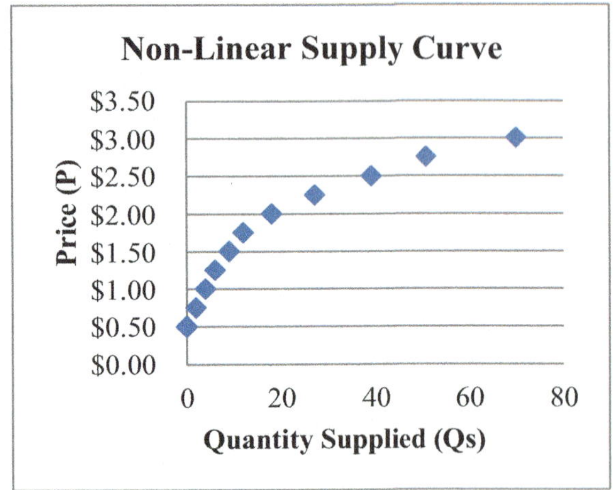

Figure 8b. Nonlinear supply curve

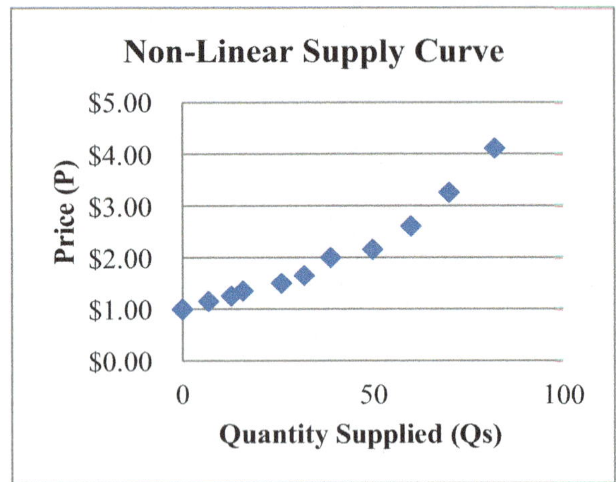

UNDERSTANDING EQUILIBRIUM:

There are competing interests for any given product or service. If consumers prefer to pay a low price and suppliers prefer to charge a high price, what price will that product or service be supplied and sold for? In other words, what will the equilibrium price be whereby quantity demanded equals quantity supplied (i.e., Qd = Qs)?

In continuing with the Twix chocolate bars example, on a graph, we can overlay the demand curve on top of the supply curve to see if and where the curves intersect. At the point of intersection, the quantity demanded is equal to the quantity supplied; both the consumer and the supplier are willing to buy and sell the chocolate bars at this point.

But first, we can create a combined demand and supply schedule. See figure 9.

Figure 9. Demand & supply schedule for Twix chocolate bars (per week)

Price (P)	Quantity Demanded (Qd)	Quantity Supplied (Qs)
$0.50	70	0
$0.75	63	7
$1.00	56	14
$1.25	49	21
$1.50	42	28
$1.75	35	35
$2.00	28	42
$2.25	21	49
$2.50	14	56
$2.75	7	63
$3.00	0	70

From the table in figure 9, at a price of $0.50, the consumer and the supplier are at the opposite end of the spectrum: the consumer demands 70 bars of chocolate per week, but the supplier does not wish to supply any bars of chocolate at all. The reverse can be said at a price of $3.00. It is only at a price of $1.75 where an agreement from both parties is reached. Both the consumer and the supplier are willing to buy and sell 35 Twix chocolate bars per week at a price of $1.75 per bar.

Visually, if we were to overlay the demand and supply curve on one graph, we would be able to see the point of intersection occur at a price of $1.75. (As an exercise, you may want to open an Excel spreadsheet; input the price, quantity demanded, and quantity supplied numbers from figure

9; and create a line graph. Can you see the demand and supply curves intersect at a price of $1.75 and at a quantity of 35?)

Can equilibrium always be found? The answer is no. From a consumer's perspective, what if you didn't like Twix chocolate or you felt the price of $1.75 per bar was too high? In that case, an equilibrium condition would not be met; you would not buy the chocolate, and thus, not enter or engage in the market for Twix chocolate bars. From a supplier's perspective, what if you felt $1.75 was too low of a price to adequately compensate you to supply the product? Again, in that case, no equilibrium condition would be met as you would not sell the Twix chocolate bars for $1.75. See figure 10 for a graphical example where equilibrium is not found (i.e., where the demand and the supply curves do not intersect).

Figure 10. Demand & supply (no market equilibrium)

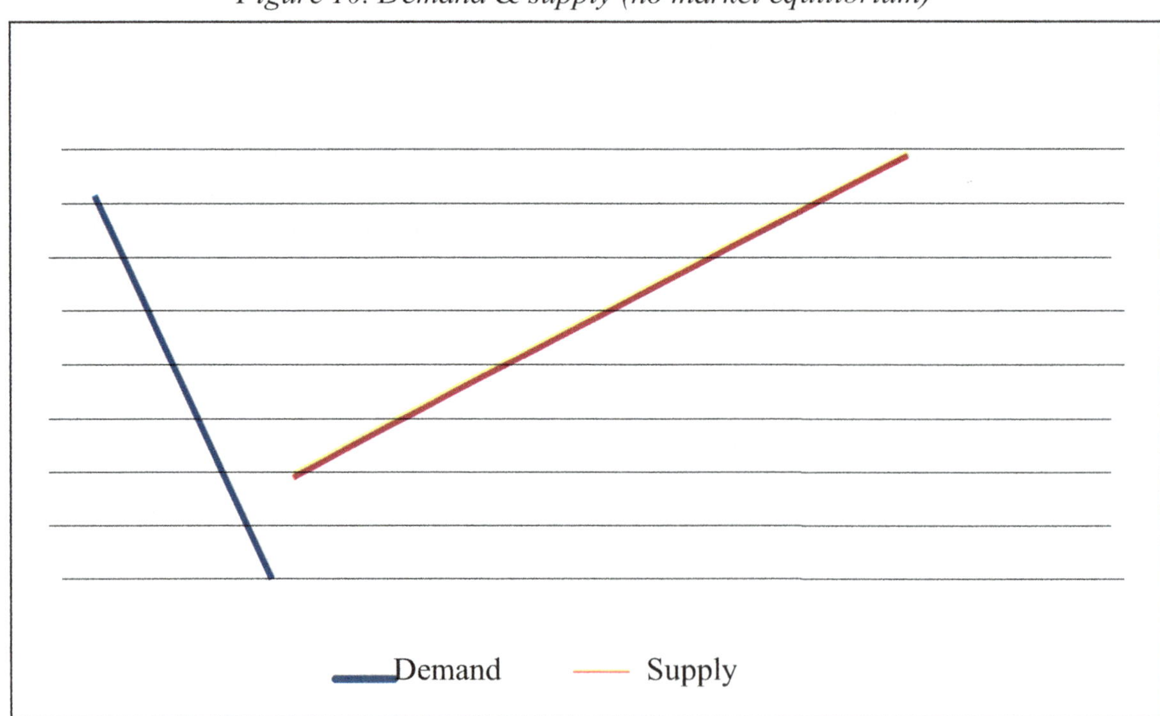

Now, what if an equilibrium condition exists but is unknown to the economic participants? From a consumer perspective, this may lead to paying more for a product/service or not purchasing the product/service at all! From a producer perspective, in Chapter 5, we will look at what happens in the market when a supplier sets the price above and when the supplier sets the price below the market equilibrium. However, suffice it to say that prices will not be stable and will fluctuate unless an equilibrium condition is met. Remember, market equilibrium is only attained when Qd = Qs!

MARKET DEMAND & SUPPLY EQUILIBRIUM:

After gaining an understanding of the individual demand curve, we can now focus our attention to the market demand curve. The market demand curve is the sum of every individual demand curve's quantity demanded at a particular price.

Figure 11 is a table representing four individual consumers' demand for Twix chocolate bars. If we assume that there are only four consumers in this market, then the market demand for this chocolate is simply the sum of each quantity demanded per consumer at each price.

Figure 11. Market demand schedule for Twix chocolate bars (per week)

Price	Consumer 1	Quantity Consumer 2	Demanded Consumer 3	Consumer 4	Market Demand
$0.50	22	34	33	10	99
$0.75	20	31	30	9	90
$1.00	18	28	27	8	81
$1.25	16	25	24	7	72
$1.50	14	22	21	6	63
$1.75	12	19	18	5	54
$2.00	10	16	15	4	45
$2.25	8	13	12	3	36
$2.50	6	10	9	2	27
$2.75	4	7	6	1	18
$3.00	2	4	3	0	9

As seen in figure 11, the market demand is the horizontal addition of the four quantities that are demanded for each of the four consumers. Accordingly, at a price of $2.75, we add four chocolate bars per week that would be demanded from Consumer 1, plus seven chocolate bars per week that would be demanded from Consumer 2, plus six bars of chocolate per week that would be demanded from Consumer 3, plus one bar of chocolate per week that would be demanded from Consumer 4. This sums up to 18 bars of Twix chocolate per week that would be demanded at a price of $2.75. Thus, at a price of $2.75, the market demand for Twix would equal 18 total bars of chocolate per week.

After understanding an individual firm's supply curve, we can now focus our attention to the market supply curve. The market supply curve, similar to the market demand curve, is the sum of every individual supply curve's quantity supplied at a particular price.

Figure 12 is a table representing two individual firms' supply of Twix chocolate bars. If we assume that there are only two suppliers of Twix chocolate in this market, then the market supply of this chocolate is simply the sum of each quantity supplied per firm at each price.

Figure 12. Market supply schedule for Twix chocolate bars (per week)

	Quantity Supplied		
Price	Firm 1	Firm 2	Market Supply
$0.50	5	10	15
$0.75	7	13	20
$1.00	9	16	25
$1.25	11	19	30
$1.50	13	22	35
$1.75	15	25	40
$2.00	17	28	45
$2.25	19	31	50
$2.50	21	34	55
$2.75	23	37	60
$3.00	25	40	65

As seen in figure 12, the market supply is the horizontal addition of the two quantities that are supplied for each of the two suppliers. Accordingly, at a price of $2.75, we add 23 chocolate bars per week that would be supplied from Firm 1 plus 37 chocolate bars per week that would be supplied from Firm 2. This sums up to 60 Twix chocolate bars per week that would be supplied at a price of $2.75. Thus, at a price of $2.75, the market supply for Twix will be 60 total bars of chocolate per week.

Looking at both the market demand and the market supply schedules in our fictitious neighborhood, if we assume there are only four consumers whose demand for Twix chocolate bars follows the quantity demanded as shown in figure 11, and we assume there are only two firms whose supply for Twix chocolates follows the quantity supplied as shown in figure 12, can we find the market equilibrium? Yes—to find the market equilibrium, we need to ask, at what price will the market demand equal the market supply? From the table in figure 12, we can note that the new market equilibrium price will be set at $2.00; at this price, Qd = Qs = 45 Twix chocolate bars per week.

Graphically, the market demand and market supply curves for Twix chocolate bars are shown in figure 13.

Figure 13. Market equilibrium graph for Twix chocolate bars (per week)

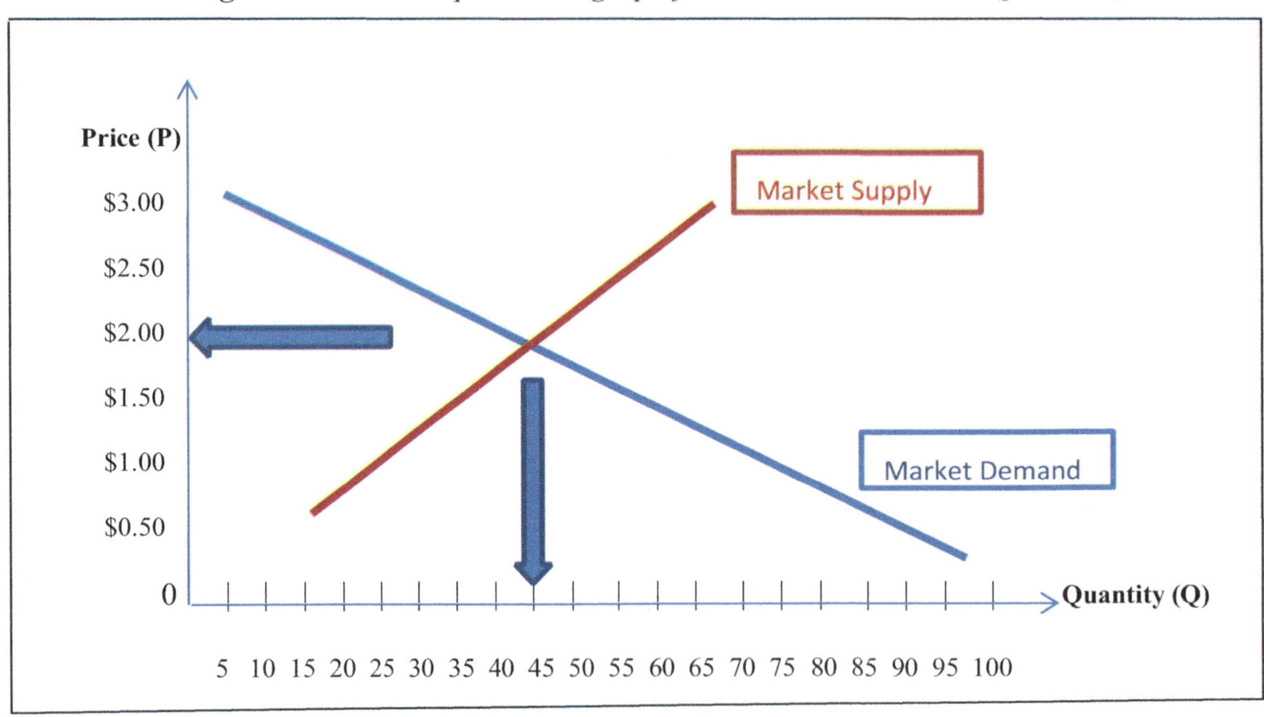

Note that in this case, the demand and supply curves are linear. However, at each price, the changes in demand and in supply are not the same. In other words, the slope of the demand curve is different than the slope of the supply curve. This leads us to the discussion about the significance of slopes in Chapter 3.

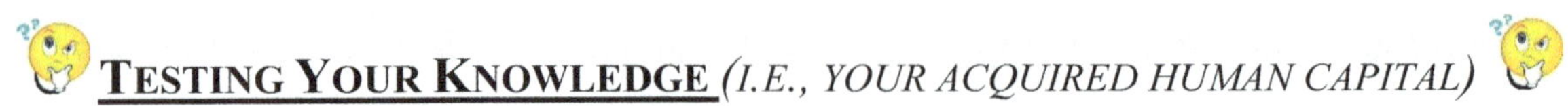

TESTING YOUR KNOWLEDGE *(I.E., YOUR ACQUIRED HUMAN CAPITAL)*

Determine whether the following statements are true or false. If false, can you explain why?

1. All demand curves are linear.
2. For a supplier, the higher the price, the less the firm is willing to supply.
3. An equilibrium condition always exists in the market.
4. The market demand represents the average quantity demanded of all the participants at a particular price.
5. When graphing a demand curve, the demand for the product/service is measured along the X-axis.

CHAPTER 3. CLASSIFICATION OF GOODS, SLOPE & ELASTICITY

In the previous chapter, we discussed that the market for goods and services follows the law of demand (from the consumer perspective) and the law of supply (from the producer perspective). But do the laws of demand and supply hold true for all types of goods and services? Naturally, goods and services are priced differently based upon several factors. But, given a particular category of goods or services (e.g., jeans or tax preparers, respectively), are all goods and services within each category perceived to be of equal value? In other words, do consumers perceive all jeans or all tax preparers to be of equal value? Before answering these questions, we must look at the classification of goods and services.

CLASSIFICATION OF GOODS/SERVICES & THEIR EFFECT ON DEMAND:

Goods and services can be classified into three categories: normal, superior/luxury, and inferior.

A "normal" good or service is one that is commonly or normally used in everyday life. More specifically, a normal good/service exhibits the following property: as real[8] incomes rise, the demand for that good/service also rises; and as real incomes fall, the demand for that good/service also falls. Examples of a normal good include food staples, household appliances, and clothing.

What is considered a "superior" or a "luxury" good/service may be debated at times given different customs, cultures, and economic standings. However, the consensus is that luxury goods/services are those that are not "must-haves" or necessities. See figure 1 for examples of luxury items. The

[8] We insert the term "real" before the word "incomes" as we are referring to the after-inflation adjustment in incomes. We will discuss this concept in more detail in Chapter 9.

following is a short list of examples that are considered superior services: education at a private institution; tax returns prepared by a licensed tax preparer who also holds a CPA license; medical treatment from a nurse with a DNP degree; and college accounting classes taught by an instructor who holds both a CPA and a PhD in accounting.

In sum, for a luxury good or service, the higher an individual's real income, the larger his/her share of income is devoted to the purchase of superior/luxury goods or services. Does this category of goods and services follow the law of demand? The answer is yes! As real incomes rise, individuals will want to purchase higher-priced (i.e., considered to be luxury) goods or services. Thus, the demand for those products rises. And when real incomes decrease, on average, individuals will purchase fewer luxury items. Thus, the demand for luxury items drops.

Figure 1. Examples of luxury vs. inferior goods

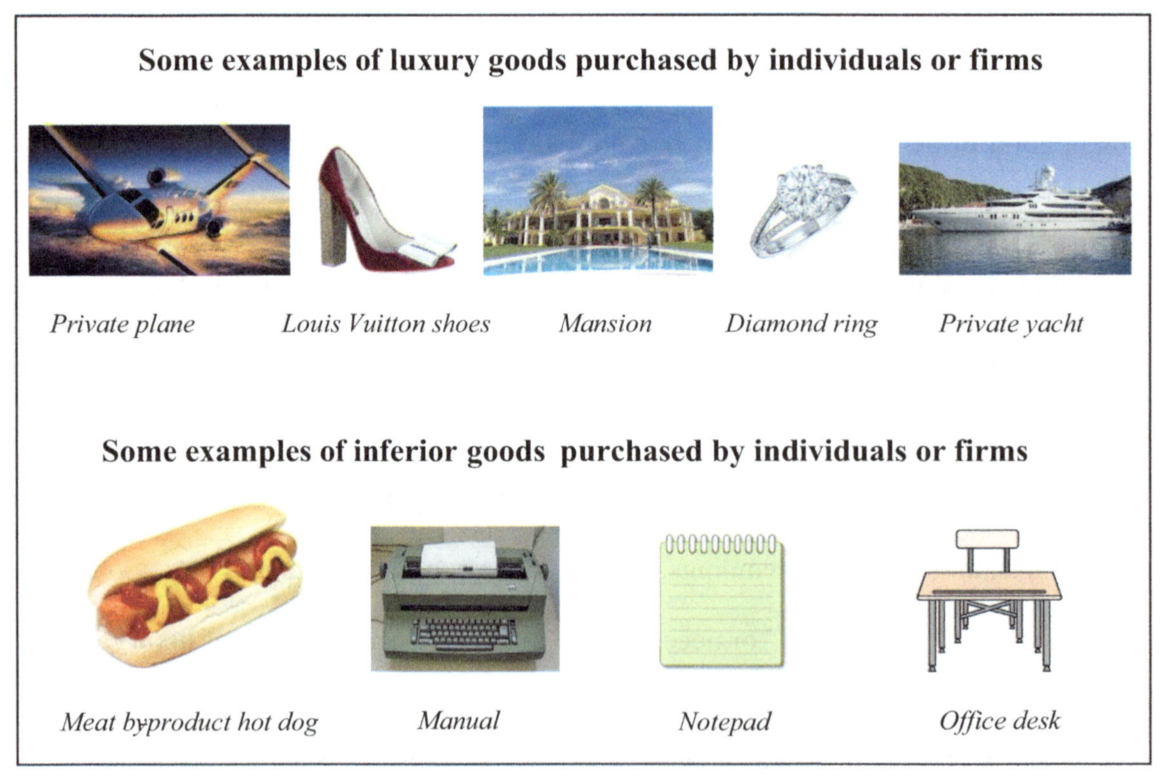

Once again, what is considered an "inferior" good or service may be debated at times given different customs, cultures, and economic standings; but the consensus is that an inferior good will not be purchased (or will be purchased less) when real incomes rise. So, the higher a consumer's real income, the lower their demand for inferior goods or services. This is because consumers will switch from "inferior" products to "normal" products. See figure 1 for examples of inferior goods. As real incomes rise, consumers may switch from these inferior products to their "normal" alternatives: all-beef franks, computers, tablets, and larger desks with drawers.

But what are examples of inferior services? The following is a short list of examples that are considered inferior services: education at a school that is not accredited; tax returns prepared by an unlicensed tax preparer; a haircut by your 13-year-old sibling; electrical rewiring done by an unlicensed electrician; a manicure done by a friend; and videography, and photography performed by nonprofessionals in their respective fields.

To better understand the difference between a luxury, normal, and inferior product or service, figure 2 offers comparative examples for each category.

Figure 2. Examples of goods & services by categorization

Luxury	Normal	Inferior
Nurse with a DNP or NP degree	Registered nurse	Nurse assistant or medical assistant
Filet mignon steak	Sirloin steak	Chuck steak
Valentino or Burberry brand products	Adidas or Polo brand products	Off-brand (e.g., from Target) products
Natural AAA-grade pearls	Cultured AA-grade pearls	Simulated/faux A-grade pearls
Moët or Dom Pérignon champagne	Perrier-Jouët or Drappier champagne	Korbel or sparkling wine champagne
N/A	Coca-Cola	C&C Cola or Waldbaum's Cola
N/A	Bayer aspirin	Rite Aid aspirin
Private health care	Employer-sponsored health care	Government-sponsored health care
Babysitter with a college degree in child adolescence	18-plus-year-old babysitter with no degree in child adolescence	13-year-old babysitter

For each of the three categories of goods and services, we can use the following table (fig. 3) to sum up what happens to the demand for a product when real incomes rise.

Figure 3. Types of good, income & demand relationships

Type of Good	Real Incomes	Demand
Luxury Good	↑	↑
	↓	↓
Normal Good	↑	↑
	↓	↓
Inferior Good	↑	↓
	↓	↑

THE SLOPE, ITS MEASURE & ITS MEANING:

What is a slope and why do we measure it? A slope is calculated as the change (or difference) in what is being measured, in units, on the vertical axis divided by the change (or difference) in what is being measured, in units, on the horizontal axis. This is often referred to as a change in the rise over the change in the run; or the change in Y over the change in X).[9]

$$\text{slope} = (Y_1 - Y_2) / (X_1 - X_2) \qquad (1.1)$$

$$= (P_1 - P_2) / (Qd_1 - Qd_2)$$

[9] In mathematical terms, the slope is the "m" in the function "Y = mX + b." In regression analysis, the slope is the "β_1" in the function "$Y = \beta_o + \beta_1 X_1 + e$."

Let's continue with our Twix chocolate bar example from Chapter 2 (Figure 3). As the price of one chocolate bar changed by twenty-five cents, the quantity demanded changed by seven units (chocolate bars) per week. This can be seen in figure 4, where the demand schedule is reproduced, and a change is calculated for the price and quantity demanded at each two points.

Figure 4. Demand schedule for Twix chocolate bars (per week)-changes in P & Qd

Change (Increase) in Price	Price	Quantity Demanded	Change (Decrease) in Quantity Demanded
Price increases by \$0.25—from \$0.50 to \$0.75.	\$0.50	70	Quantity decreases by 7 units—from 70 to 63.
	\$0.75	63	
Etc.	\$1.00	56	
Price increases by \$0.25—from \$1.00 to \$1.25.	\$1.25	49	Etc.
Etc.	\$1.50	42	Quantity decreases by 7 units—from 42 to 35.
Price increases by \$0.25—from \$1.50 to \$1.75.	\$1.75	35	
Etc.	\$2.00	28	Etc.
	\$2.25	21	Quantity decreases by 7 units—from 21 to 14.
Price increases by \$0.25—from \$2.50 to \$2.75.	\$2.50	14	
	\$2.75	7	Etc.
	\$3.00	0	

As the changes in both price and quantity demanded are constant (i.e., as the units in price always change by twenty-five cents and the units in quantity demanded always change by seven bars), the slope will be constant (i.e., will not change). Plugging these numbers into equation (1.1), we can find the slope by dividing the change in price by the change in quantity demanded:

$0.25 / -7 = -0.03571. The slope is negative (which makes sense as price and quantity demanded follow the law of demand) and can be seen graphed in Chapter 2 (fig. 4).[10]

But you may ask, what if I wanted to know the slope from a price change of $0.50 to $2.00 (that is, not the change between two sequential price differences)? Will the slope still be -0.03571? The answer is yes. Here is the mathematical proof: the change (i.e., difference) from $0.50 to $2.00 is an increase in price of $1.50. The corresponding quantity demanded at $0.50 is 70 units, and the corresponding quantity demanded at $2.00 is 28 units; so, the difference is a decrease of 42 units (i.e., 70 – 28 = 42).

Once again, we can apply the slope formula from equation (1.1):

$$\begin{aligned} \text{slope} &= (\$0.50 - \$2.00) / (70 - 28) \\ &= -\$1.50 / 42 \\ &= -0.03571 \end{aligned}$$

The "beauty" (in mathematics, called the "property") of a linear curve is that the slope is always constant. Therefore, you may measure the slope given any two points of the X and corresponding Y variables and it will always be the same.

---

[10] Note, in regression analysis, if you regress price and quantity demanded where X = quantity demanded and Y = price, your regression output will be $Y = 84 - 0.03571 \times X$. The beta coefficient on Price, β_1, will be -0.03571 (the slope of the function).

We can apply the same process in calculating the slope of the supply curve. Can you guess what the sign of the supply curve will be (i.e., will it be negative or positive)? From Chapter 2 (fig. 6), as the price of one Twix chocolate bar changed by $0.25, the quantity supplied changed by 7 units. If you wanted to know the slope of the supply curve from a price of $0.50 to $3.00, the corresponding quantities supplied at these prices are 0 and 70 units respectively. Apply the slope formula from equation (1.1):

slope = ($0.50 – $3.00) / (0 – 70)

= -$2.50 / -70

= 0.03571

Did you guess the sign of the slope of the supply curve correctly? Great! The slope is now positive following the law of supply and as evidenced when graphed in Chapter 2 (fig. 7).

Please take notice: if the curve is <u>not</u> linear, the slope will change among any two points. The following examples are taken from the nonlinear demand and supply curves from Chapter 2 (figs. 5 and 8*b*, respectfully).

<u>Scenario from the Demand Schedule Graphed from Chapter 2, Figure 5</u>

Example 1: The slope of a price change from $3.00 to $2.00 with corresponding changes in quantities demanded from 0 and 9 is equal to **-0.1111**

(i.e., [$3 – $2] / [0 – 9] = $1 / -9 = -0.1111).

Example 2: However, the slope of a price change from $1.50 to $0.50 with corresponding changes in quantities demanded from 18 and 70 is equal to **-0.0192**

(i.e., [$1.50 – $0.50] / [18 – 70] = $1.00 / -52 = -0.0192).

As you can see, in this scenario, the slope is not constant. It changes from -0.1111 to -0.0192. While the slope is negative in both examples, the slope is flatter (i.e., in absolute values, a smaller number—as 0.0192 < 0.1111) in Example 2.

<u>Scenario from the Supply Schedule Graphed from Chapter 2, Figure 8a</u>

Example 1: The slope of a price change from $0.75 to $1.50 with corresponding changes in quantities demanded from 2 and 9 is equal to **0.1071**

(i.e., [$0.75 – $1.50] / [2 – 9] = -$0.75 / -7 = 0.1071).

Example 2: However, the slope of a price change from $2.25 to $3 with corresponding changes in quantities demanded from 27 and 70 is equal to **0.0174**

(i.e., [$2.25 – $3.00] / [27 – 70] = -$0.75 / -43 = 0.0174).

As you can see, the slope is not constant: 0.1071 versus 0.0174. While the slope is now positive in both examples, the slope is steeper (i.e., in absolute values, a larger number) in Example 1.

IMPORTANCE OF A SLOPE & PRACTICAL EXAMPLES:

In practical terms, what is the importance of the slope? What does it tell us? Why do we bother calculating it? In everyday usage, the slope tells us the marginal (or additional) effect or impact one variable has upon the other. Let's say we jotted down the number of hours spent doing a homework assignment and the corresponding grade (in points out of 100) received on that assignment. In this case, the Y variable will represent the overall grade in points received on the assignment and the X variable will represent the number of hours spent studying. Assuming the relationship between the number of hours spent on the assignment and the grade is positive (i.e., the higher the number of hours spent on the assignment, the higher the grade) and assuming this relationship is linear, the slope would tell us that for every additional hour spent doing the assignment, the grade will increase by the calculated slope. So, if the calculated slope equaled 10.325, this would mean that for every additional hour spent studying, on average, the overall assignment grade increases by 10.325 points (out of 100 points).

Another application of the slope function would be if a business firm tried to ascertain (1) whether increased marketing led to increased sales and (2) for each additional dollar spent on marketing, how much did sales increase by? In trying to answer these answers, the firm captured its weekly sales and marketing expenses for 26 weeks. If the firm assumed a constant (or quasi-constant) slope, they could calculate the marginal/incremental impact an additional dollar of advertising would affect sales by applying the slope formula from equation (1.1): (sales week 1 – sales week 26) / (advertising dollars week 1 – advertising dollars week 26). If this formula resulted in a calculated value of 142.8924, what would this mean?

Was it worth spending the advertising money? To directly answer the firm's first question, yes; the slope is positive, so increased marketing did lead to increased sales. To directly answer the firm's second question, the slope tells us that for each additional dollar spent on advertising, on average, sales increased by $142.89. So, is this marketing campaign worth the effort? Numerically, yes, but what about the effort and time spent in carrying out the marketing campaign? This, naturally, is a business decision that a simple slope calculation alone cannot answer; it will need further exploration!

ELASTICITY, ITS MEASUREMENT & ITS MEANING:

Most often, the elasticity of a good/service is measured to gauge what happens to quantity demanded/supplied in relation to changes in price or income; these measurements are referred to as price elasticity of demand (PED) or income elasticity of demand (IED), respectively.

The price elasticity of demand is used to assess the degree to which all participants (i.e., individuals, consumers, or producers), as a percentage, change their quantity demanded for a product/service when the price of a good or service changes. The income elasticity of demand is used to assess the degree to which all participants, as a percentage, change their quantity demanded/supplied when income changes.

Elasticity is calculated as the percentage change in what is being measured, in units, on the horizontal axis divided by the percentage change in what is being measured, in units, on the vertical axis; or, the percentage change in X over the percentage change in Y[11]. In other words,

$$\text{elasticity} = \%\text{ change in X} / \%\text{ change in Y}$$

$$\textit{or,} \quad = [(X_1 - X_2) / X_2] / [(Y_1 - Y_2) / Y_2]$$

We will discuss each of these two elasticities, PED and IED, in turn.

---

[11] Note, in comparing equation 1.1 of the slope formula to equation 1.2 of the elasticity formula, the variables in the numerator and denominator are reversed.

How to Measure & Interpret the Price Elasticity of Demand (PED):

$$PED = [(Qd_1 - Qd_2) / Qd_2] / [(P_1 - P_2) / P_2] \quad (1.2)$$

Where, Qd_1 = new quantity demanded

Qd_2 = old quantity demanded

P_1 = new price

And, P_2 = old price

In practical terms, what is the importance of the elasticity formula? What does it tell us? Why do we bother calculating it?

Say you are the manufacturer of a product and you want to know what would happen to the quantity demanded of that product if you increased its price. Using the demand schedule created in Chapter 2 (fig. 4) as the example, you know that the demand curve is linear. You also know that the slope, given equation (1.1) and as calculated previously = -0.03571. In other words, in order to sell one additional quantity (i.e., unit), the price will have to decrease by approximately four cents.

But knowing the slope does not answer your question: how sensitive are your current consumers to the price of this product? If you are thinking about increasing your price from $2.00 to $2.50, you know the quantity demanded will drop from 28 units to 14 units, respectively. So, over this upper range of prices for Twix chocolate bars, how will an increase in price affect consumers' quantity demanded?

Employing equation (1.2), we can calculate the price elasticity of demand as follows:

$$PED = [(Qd_1 - Qd_2) / Qd_2] / [(P_1 - P_2) / P_2]$$
$$= [(28 - 14) / 14] / [(2.00 - 2.50) / 2.50]$$
$$= 1 / -0.20$$
$$= -5$$

What this means is that if you were to change the price (i.e., the denominator in the formula) of your product by 1%, this will inversely (as the sign is negative) cause the quantity demanded (i.e., the numerator in the formula) to change by 5%.[12] In this scenario, a 1% increase in price will cause a 5% drop in quantity demanded. (Conversely, if you dropped your price by 1%, this will result in a 5% increase in quantity demanded!) In absolute values, as the percentage change in price < percentage change in quantity demanded (i.e., 0.20 < 1), the price elasticity of demand is greater than one (i.e., equal to 5). Therefore, the price elasticity of demand is viewed as "elastic"; very sensitive to prices—especially over the higher range of prices for Twix chocolate bars.

So, how will this affect your business' total revenue? Total revenue is calculated as the sum of price multiplied by quantity demanded, symbolically expressed as $\sum(P \times Qd)$. As an example, assume you are an employee and asked to open the store one morning which had $0 in the cash register. Also assume that all the items in the store were priced at $1.00. After you served two customers, your boss comes into the store and asks, "how much money is in the cash register"? What he is asking is the amount of total revenue. Without opening the cash register, you remember that the first customer purchased 3 items and the second customer purchased 9 items. Therefore,

[12] Please note that if you had regressed price and quantity demanded where Y = quantity demanded and X = price, your beta coefficient of price would equal -28: the slope of the function, not the elasticity!

you quickly respond, "$12". Mathematically, the calculation you made in your head, can be written as 3 items @ $1 plus 9 items @ $1, or total revenue = $\sum(P \times Qd) = (\$1 \times 3) + (\$1 \times 9) = \$12$.

Getting back to the scenario where the PED = -5, this is great news if you are looking to lower your prices (as you will be increasing your total revenue—a decrease in price with a larger increase in quantity demanded)! However, this is extremely bad news if you intend to increase prices, as it will lead to a decrease in total revenue.

But what if you are thinking about increasing your price from $1.00 to $1.25? From the demand schedule, you know the quantity demanded will drop from 56 units to 49 units, respectively. Over this lower range of Twix prices, how will an increase in price affect consumers' quantity demanded?

Once again, employing equation (1.2), we can calculate the price elasticity of demand as follows:

$$PED = [(Qd_1 - Qd_2) / Qd_2] / [(P_1 - P_2) / P_2]$$

$$= [(56 - 49) / 49] / [(1.00 - 1.25) / 1.25]$$

$$= 0.142857 / -0.20$$

$$= -0.714285$$

What this means is that a 1% change in price will cause a 0.71% change in the quantity demanded for this product. Over the lower Twix price range, the price elasticity of demand is less than one in absolute value (i.e., 0.714285). Therefore, the price elasticity of demand is viewed as "inelastic" (i.e., not very sensitive to prices) as the absolute value of the percentage change in price > percentage change in quantity demanded. This is great news if you are looking to increase your prices. But it is extremely bad news if you intend to decrease prices (as you will be decreasing your total revenue—a decrease in price with little increase in quantity demanded)!

In the previous two examples, we saw a scenario whereby the absolute value of the PED was less than 1 and a scenario whereby the absolute value of the PED was greater than 1. Can the PED be equal to one? And, if so, what does this imply about the relationship between price and its quantity demanded?

If the price elasticity of demand is equal to one in absolute value, this means that the percentage change in quantity demanded equals the percentage change in price, or $[(Qd_1 – Qd_2) / Qd_2] = [(P_1 – P_2) / P_2]$ utilizing equation 1.2. Therefore, the price elasticity of demand is viewed as "unit elastic"; fluctuations in price will be accompanied by the same percentage change in the quantity demanded of a good/service. In this case, increasing or decreasing your prices will have no impact on your total revenue, as you will experience the same percentage change decrease or increase (respectively) in quantity demanded.

From these examples, we can conclude the following properties about the calculated values of the price elasticity of demand:

1. If the price elasticity of demand is greater than 1, irrespective of its sign, we say the demand is "elastic." Applying the elasticity formula (1.2), this means that a 1% change (where mathematically, the symbol for change is "Δ") in price will cause a greater percentage change in the quantity demanded for this product. This is the result we saw in the previous example (where EOD = -5) when measuring the price elasticity of demand over the higher price range for Twix chocolate bars. Again, this is great news if you are

looking to lower the item's price but bad news if you intend to increase it! Symbolically, we can say: a $\% \Delta Qd > \% \Delta P$. As a result, *ceteris paribus*, a price increase will lower total revenues and a price decrease will increase total revenues. Remember, total revenue $= \sum(P \times Qd)$.

2. If the price elasticity of demand is less than 1, irrespective of its sign, we say the demand is "inelastic." Applying the elasticity formula from equation (1.2), this means that a 1% change in price will cause a lesser percentage change in the quantity demanded for this product. This is the result we saw in the previous example (where the EOD = -0.714285) when measuring the price elasticity of demand over the lower price range for Twix chocolate bars. Again, this is great news if you are looking to increase the item's price but bad news if you intend to decrease it! Symbolically, we can say: a $\% \Delta Qd < \% \Delta P$. As a result, *ceteris paribus*, a price increase will increase total revenues and a price decrease will decrease total revenues.

3. If the price elasticity of demand is equal to 1, irrespective of its sign, we say the demand is "unit elastic." This means that the percentage change in quantity demanded is equal to the percentage change in price. Applying the elasticity formula from equation (1.2), this means that a 1% change in price will cause a 1% change in the quantity demanded for this product. Symbolically, we can say, a $\% \Delta Qd = \% \Delta P$. As a result, *ceteris paribus*, a price increase or decrease will have no impact on total revenues.

The table in figure 5 offers some examples of products that fall under each of the price elasticity of demand categories.

Figure 5. Products/services according to their price elasticity of demand (PED)

Elastic **(PED > |1|)**	**Unit Elastic** **(PED = |1|)**	**Inelastic** **(PED < |1|)**
In practice, these are products/services that have many substitutes, so they are price sensitive. Examples include: chocolate bars, soups, costume jewelry, cookies, T-shirts, and airline tickets for vacation travel.	In practice, there are no products or services that are exactly unit elastic. A close proxy would be products or services that have close substitutes or alternatives, like clothing, fresh fish, and soda products.	In practice, these are products/services that have very little substitutes, so they are not price sensitive. Examples include: cigarettes, gasoline, salt, medicine, heating oil, diamonds, and specialized surgeons.

How to Measure & Interpret the Income Elasticity of Demand (IED):

Similar in format to the PED formula, IED is calculated as follows:

$$IED = [(Qd_1 - Qd_2) / Qd_2] / [(I_1 - I_2) / I_2], \qquad (1.3)$$

Where, Qd_1 = new quantity demanded

Qd_2 = old quantity demanded

I_1 = new income

And, I_2 = old income

In practical terms, what is the importance of the income elasticity formula? What does it tell us? Why do we bother calculating it? In relation to the income elasticity of demand, we ask, how sensitive is the demand for a product when income changes?

If we were to employ equation (1.3) in determining the income elasticity of demand for goods and services, we would note the following for each of the goods/services categories:

1. A **normal good** has an income elasticity of demand that is positive but less than one. For example, if income increases by 10% and quantity demanded increases by 5%, then the IED equals 0.5. (Symbolically, we can write, $\% \Delta Qd < \% \Delta I$ where "I" represents "income".) As stated previously under the classification of goods, as income rises, the demand for normal products/services increases (i.e., the demand curve shifts to the right[13]). So, given that the price for a normal product/service has not changed, the quantity demanded of that product/service will increase. Conversely, if incomes fall, the demand for the product/service will decrease (i.e., the demand curve shifts to the left[14]). So, given that the price for the product/service has not changed, the quantity demanded of that good/service will decrease. In either case, for a normal good, the change in quantity demanded will be less than the change in income. Generally speaking, this means that when the economy is in a recession and, on average, incomes fall, the quantities demanded of normal goods will also fall but by a lesser percentage; the opposite is also true.

2. A **luxury good** has an income elasticity of demand that is positive but greater than one. For example, if income increases by 10% and quantity demanded increases by 18%, then the IED equals 1.8. (Symbolically, we can write, $\% \Delta Qd > \% \Delta I$.) As stated previously under the classification of goods, as incomes rise, the demand for luxury products/services increases (i.e., the demand curve shifts to the right). So, given that the price for a luxury product/service has not changed, the quantity demanded of that product/service will increase, and vice versa. In either case, for a luxury good, the change in quantity demanded will be greater than the change in income. Generally speaking, this means that when the

[13] See Chapter 4: The Five Determinants of Demand.

[14] Ibid.

economy is in a recession and, on average, incomes fall, the quantities demanded of luxury goods will also fall but by a greater percentage; the opposite is also true. Therefore, firms that produce luxury goods are more susceptible to economic fluctuations; they grow more rapidly during economic booms and shrink more rapidly during economic busts!

3. An **inferior good** has an income elasticity of demand that is negative. For example, if income increases by 10% and the quantity demanded decreases by 3%, then the IED equals -0.3. [Symbolically, we can write, (% Δ Qd / % Δ I) < 0.] As stated previously under the classification of goods, as incomes rise, the demand for inferior products/services decreases (i.e., the demand curve shifts to the left). So, given that the price for an inferior product/service has not changed, the quantity demanded of that good/service will decrease. Conversely, if incomes fall, the demand for the product/service will increase (i.e., the demand curve shifts to the right). So, given that the price for the product/service has not changed, the quantity demanded of that good/service will increase. In either case, for an inferior good, the change in quantity demanded divided by the change in income will be negative. Generally speaking, this means that when the economy is in a recession and, on average, incomes fall, the quantities demanded of inferior goods will rise; the opposite is also true. Therefore, firms that produce inferior goods are more susceptible to economic fluctuations; they grow more rapidly during economic busts and shrink more rapidly during economic booms!

Now that you have a better understanding of elasticity, if you owned or managed a business, what would you prefer the price elasticity of demand and income elasticity of demand for your product or service to be? Why?

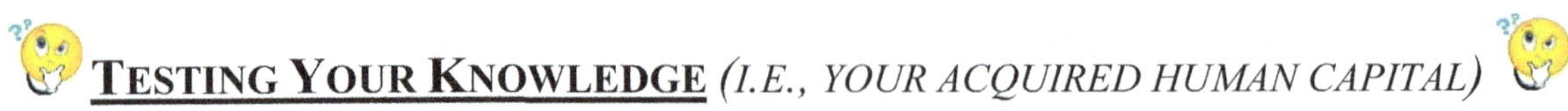

Determine whether the following statements are true or false. If false, can you explain why?

1. An inferior good is a good for which when real income rises, you purchase less of that product.
2. If the income elasticity of a good has been calculated to be 0.79, we can infer that the good is considered a normal good.
3. If the percentage change in quantity demanded is greater than the percentage change in price, we would say that, over this range, demand is elastic.
4. If the percentage change in quantity demanded is equal to the percentage change in price (in absolute values), then an increase in price will result in no change in total revenue.
5. Suppose a consumer's income increases from $45,000 to $60,000. As a result, the consumer increases his/her purchase of video games from 15 to 20 video games[15] per year. The consumer's income elasticity of demand for video games is equal to one; therefore, video games are considered a normal good and its elasticity is unit elastic!

[15] According to data from the NPD Group (Video Games Market Research & Business Solutions, 2017), the amount of video game software sold in 2012 was $6.7 billion, or 174.8 million units. By the third quarter of 2018, NPD reported that the total industry consumer spending on video games was $9.1 billion.

CHAPTER 4. NEW EQUILIBRIUM: SHIFTS IN DEMAND & SUPPLY

In Chapter 2, we discussed static (i.e., nonmoving) equilibrium price and quantity when we overlaid demand and supply curves on one graph. But do the demand and/or supply curves ever change? If so, how do they affect equilibrium price and quantity?

CHANGES IN DEMAND:

Once again, use the Twix chocolate bars example from Chapter 2. Regarding the demand for Twix bars, what would make that individual demand more or less Twix chocolate bars during a seven-day period at those particular prices? Can you think of some "factors" (i.e., reasons)?

For most of the population, from the consumer (or buyers') perspective, we find there are five factors (also referred as "determinants of demand") that can make the demand curve change/shift. They are tastes/preferences, income, prices of related goods, number of consumers/buyers, and expectations of future prices. In all cases, an increase in any one of these five determinants will cause the entire demand curve to increase at each price level—the demand curve will shift to the right; see figure 1 for a graphical look at this increase in demand.

Figure 1. Increase in demand

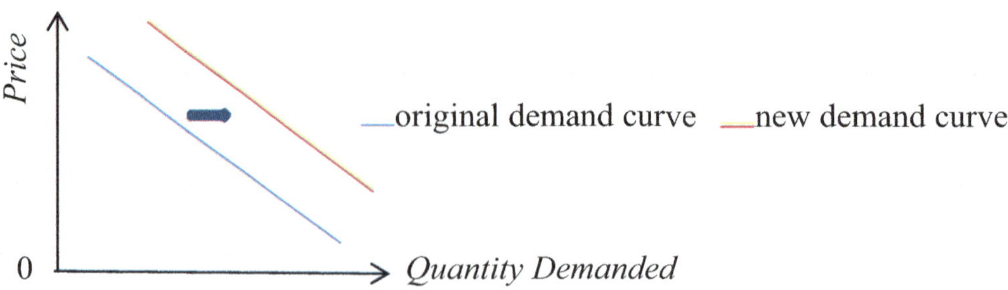

Similarly, a decrease in any one of these five determinants will cause the entire demand curve to decrease at each price level—the demand curve will shift to the left; see figure 2 for a graphical view of this decrease in demand.

Figure 2. Decrease in demand

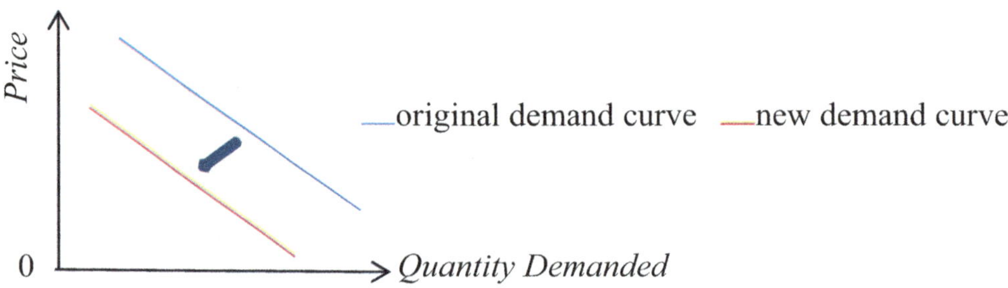

The Five "Determinants" & Their Effect on Demand:

1. Tastes/Preferences

Due to many factors, such as age, exposure to a product/service, and advertising, consumer tastes and/or preferences for a particular product or service may change. They may increase or decrease. If the taste/preference increases, the demand curve also increases (see fig. 1), and vice versa. As an example, as babies age, their taste for baby food decreases. At each price level, this causes a decrease in the demand for baby food (see fig. 2).

2. Income

As incomes rise, most consumers increase their demand for normal or luxury goods/services; as incomes decrease (due to layoffs, less overtime, retirement, etc.), most consumers decrease their demand for these products/services. As an example, on average, consumers that like to get back massages tend to purchase more (or longer) back massages as their incomes rise; thus, their demand for back massages increases (see fig. 1).

For inferior products/services, most consumers decrease their demand as their incomes rise, and vice versa. As an example, as incomes rise, consumers, on average, decrease their consumption of "off-brand" items, such as C&C Cola and Rite Aid bandages. This decrease in consumption of inferior products/services may be due to the wealth affect—an increase in spending due to their perceived increase in wealth (in this case, income)—or the perceived negative inference associated with the quality of off-brand items.

3. Prices of related goods

Related goods can be classified as either "complements" or "substitutes." A "complementary good" is a good that is demanded (i.e., purchased) at the same time as the product of interest. An example of this would be hot dogs and hot dog buns. When purchasing hot dogs (the product of interest), on average, most people will also purchase hot dog buns (the complementary good). To further this example, what if you wanted to host a barbecue party and went to the store to purchase barbecue items? At the store, you might pick up hot dogs at the expected price but then notice the price for hot dog buns had increased. Would your demand for hotdogs change? Would you purchase the same number of hot dogs and buns, or would you switch your purchase of hot dogs and buns for another barbecue food item? Most consumers faced with this decision will purchase fewer hot dogs and, ergo, less hot dog buns. So, most consumers, even when there has been no change in the price of an item of interest, will change their demand for that item based upon the price of a complementary item. An example of the demand for these two complementary products may be seen in figure 3.

Figure 3. Complementary goods scenario

	Market for Hot Dogs (Item of Interest) Ball Park Bun Size Franks, 8 ct.[16]		Market for Hot Dog Buns (Complementary Item) Ball Park Hot Dog Buns, 13 oz.[17]	
	Price	**Demand**	**Price**	**Demand**
Original Demand	$3.49	2 bags	$3.39	2 bags
Increase in Price of Complimentary Good	$3.49	1 bag	$3.99	1 bag
Decrease in Price of Complimentary Good	$3.49	3 bags	$2.89	3 bags

From figure 3, while the price of hot dogs did not change, consumers decreased their demand from two bags to one bag when the price of hot dog buns increased from $3.39 to $3.99. They decreased their demand for buns as well. (Graphically, this demand curve may look like fig. 2.) Similarly, while the price of hot dogs did not change, consumers increased their demand from two bags to three bags when the price of hot dog buns decreased from $3.39 to $2.89. They also increased their demand for hot dog buns. (Graphically, this demand curve may look like fig. 1.) Why is this important to know? Beware! Even though you (as the seller) may hold prices fixed, the demand for your product will be affected when suppliers of your product's complementary good alter their

[16] Hot Dogs, 2017.

[17] Hot Dog Buns, 2017.

prices! This can work in your favor (if they lower their prices) or work against you (if they raise their prices)!

In contrast to complementary goods, a "substitute" or "substitutable good" is a good or service that is demanded in place of a product or service of interest. The classic example of a pair of substitute goods would be the soda industry's Coke and Pepsi. On average, most people wanting to purchase Coke (the product of interest) will switch their purchase to Pepsi (the substitute good) if the price of Coke is higher. To further the barbecue party scenario, if you entered the store to buy soda and saw that Pepsi was on sale, would you buy more of the Pepsi product for your guests or would you only buy Coke? Most consumers, on average, would increase their purchase of Pepsi and decrease their purchase of Coke—even if they preferred Coke to Pepsi. Why? Because Pepsi, the substitute good, is cheaper! Figure 4 summarizes the impact on the demand for Coke when the price of Pepsi, the substitute item, changes.

Figure 4. Substitutable goods scenario

Market for Pepsi (Substitute Good)		**Market for Coke** (Product of Interest)		
Price	Demand	Price	Demand	Shift in Demand
if increase	*then* decrease	*and if* no change	*then* increases	increase *shift right*
if decrease	*then* increase	*and if* no change	*then* decreases	decrease *shift left*

Why is this important to know? While your pricing structure may not change, you need to keep an eye out for the competition! If your competitors decrease their prices, the demand for your product(s) or service(s) will decrease. And if your competitors increase their prices, the demand for your product(s) or service(s) will increase.

4. Number of consumers/buyers

As the number of consumers or buyers increases, it naturally follows that the market demand for a product or service also increases. Think about a neighborhood where more families are having children. As a result, there will be an increase in demand for baby products (such as diapers, baby bottles, and pacifiers) and services (such as babysitting and pediatric care). Similarly, when the number of consumers or buyers decreases, it follows that the market demand for the product(s) or service(s) decreases. As an example, in an aging neighborhood, there will be less of a demand for nursery schools and jungle gyms.

5. Expectations of future prices

It's safe to say that everyone has seen advertisements for upcoming sales. If you were in the market for a new pair of your favorite brand of jeans and you saw an advertisement that those jeans would be on sale next week, when would you buy the jeans? Under normal circumstances, you would, in all probability, buy the jeans next week…thus delaying your demand for jeans. If other loyal customers were to follow suit, the market demand curve for that brand of jeans would shift left—a decrease in demand (as seen in fig. 2).

If, on the other hand, you hear a rumor that your favorite brand of jeans will go up in price soon, then you will likely purchase the jeans now. Again, if other loyal customers of those jeans were to follow suit, the market demand curve for that brand of jeans would shift right—an increase in demand (as seen in fig. 1).

In sum, when there is a change to one of the five determinants of demand, the demand curve will also change accordingly. But you may ask, what happens to demand when there is a change in price? Does the demand curve shift? The answer is NO! Remember, the demand curve is drawn for a series of quantities demanded at particular prices. Therefore, an increase or decrease in price, associated with the quantity demanded at that price, is already considered in the development of the demand curve. So, a change in price is simply a "movement" along the "same" demand curve!

To conclude, why study the determinants of demand? It is of importance to note that if there is no change in supply, then an increase in demand will not only cause the new market equilibrium quantity demanded and supplied to increase (as consumers purchase more of the product) but also cause the new market equilibrium price to increase. The reverse is also true. A decrease in demand (assuming no change to the supply curve) will cause the equilibrium quantity demanded and supplied to decrease and the equilibrium price to decrease.

CHANGES IN SUPPLY:

Once again following the Twix example from Chapter 2, what factors would make that chocolate bar supplier change his/her mind? What would make that supplier produce more or less Twix bars during a seven-day period at those particular prices? Can you think of some reasons?

Similar to the determinants of demand, but this time from a producer or seller's perspective, we find there are five determinants that can make a supplier change the supply curve: technology, input prices, taxes & subsidies, number of suppliers/producers, and expectations of future prices. An increase in any one of these five determinants can cause the supply curve to increase—the supply curve will shift to the right (see fig. 5).

Figure 5. Increase in supply

Price
original supply curve
new supply curve
0
Quantity Supplied

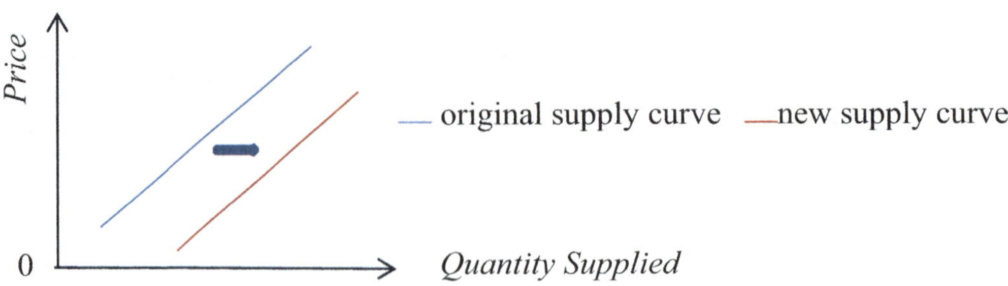

Similarly, a decrease in any one of these five determinants will cause the supply curve to decrease—the supply curve will shift to the left (see fig. 6).

Figure 6. Decrease in supply

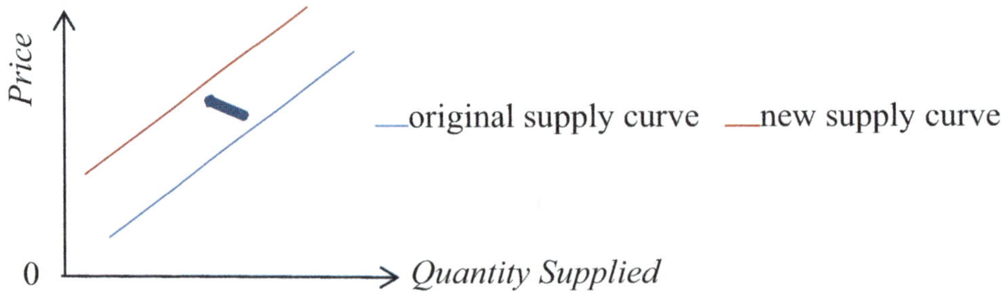

Price
original supply curve
new supply curve
0
Quantity Supplied

THE FIVE "DETERMINANTS" OF SUPPLY & THEIR EFFECT ON SUPPLY:

1. Technology

An increase in technology will lead to improved or faster production, an increase in quantity produced, and/or an improvement in quality. In essence, at every price, suppliers will be willing to, or can, supply more. As an example, from Chapter 2 (fig. 6), at a price of $1.75 suppliers would now be willing to increase their production from 35 units to 45 units; and at a price of $3, suppliers would be willing to increase their production from 70 units to 85 units. An increase in supply, at each price level, shifts the supply curve to the right (as seen in fig. 5). While technology is always improving, one can argue that there will only be an increase in supply given this determinant. However, if you see technology as a moving process, in time, technology "ages" and what used to be considered "new", in time, will be considered "old". So, a case can be made that as technology ages, there will be a decrease in the supply curve for the product using the old technology (as seen in fig. 6).

2. Input prices

Input prices include all payments that are made toward the production of a product or service. This may include wages, rent, utilities, insurance, raw materials, and more. When input prices rise (i.e., the minimum wage increases) at each price level, the overall cost of production rises. Faced with higher costs, suppliers are willing to supply less, and the supply curve will decrease (see fig. 6). When input prices fall (i.e., the price of fertilizer decreases in the production of corn), the overall cost of production decreases. Faced with lower costs, suppliers are willing to supply more, and the supply curve will increase (see fig. 5).

3. Taxes & subsidies

Similar to an increase in input prices, when the government increases taxes for a supplier, that supplier's production costs increase; therefore, the supply curve will decrease (see fig. 6). Some municipalities, to bring more businesses into the area, will reduce business taxes for new enterprises wanting to relocate to or open their business in the municipality. This reduction in taxes will entice businesses to move into that area, and, in this case, the supply curve for their product(s) or service(s) will increase (see fig. 5).

A subsidy, on the other hand, can be perceived as a negative tax; this is when the government pays a supplier less than the full cost for producing a service or a product, such as farming. A subsidy will entice the supplier to produce more; thus, the supply curve will increase (see fig. 5).

4. Number of suppliers/producers

The greater the number of suppliers or producers, the higher the supply curve (see fig. 5). The alternative is also true. As an example, due to a brush fire, with less stores in that neighborhood, fewer products will be supplied in that neighborhood. Therefore, the supply curve will decrease (see fig. 6).

5. Expectations of future prices

Suppliers, like consumers, may also be aware of the direction of future prices for the products or services they are producing. If they expect that prices of an item will increase in the future, they will be willing to supply more of that item in the future. After all, *ceteris paribus*, higher prices mean higher profits for firms! However, in the meantime, suppliers will divert their energies to producing other products/services, and the supply of the product/service in question (i.e., the product/service expected to increase in price) will decrease. Thus, the supply curve will shift to the left (see fig. 6).

In contrast, if suppliers expect prices of an item/service to decrease in the future, they will supply more of that product/service now; thus, the supply curve will shift to the right (see fig. 5).

So, why study the determinants of supply? It is of importance to note that if there is no change in demand, then an increase in supply will not only cause the new market equilibrium quantity demanded and quantity supplied to increase but also cause the new market equilibrium price to decrease. The opposite is also true.

EQUILIBRIUM CONDITIONS WITH CHANGES IN DEMAND & SUPPLY

Now that you understand what makes the demand and supply curves change (shift), what happens to the market equilibrium price and quantity when one or both curves change? Figure 7 summarizes these changes—with increases/decreases in Demand and/or Supply and the directional effect on the equilibrium price and quantity.

Figure 7. Reaching new market equilibrium with shifts in demand & supply

Combinations	Demand	Supply	Equilibrium Price	Equilibrium Quantity
A	↑	No Change	↑	↑
B	↑	↑	Indeterminate	↑
C	↑	↓	↑	Indeterminate
D	No Change	↑	↓	↑
E	No Change	↓	↑	↓
F	↓	No Change	↓	↓
G	↓	↑	↓	Indeterminate
H	↓	↓	Indeterminate	↓

As you can see in figure 7 (combinations A, D, E, and F), when only one curve changes, the equilibrium quantity will shift in the same direction of the affected curve. So, when only the demand (or the supply) curve increases, the equilibrium quantity (and thus supply) also increases. And when only the demand (or the supply) curve decreases, the equilibrium quantity (and thus supply) also decreases.

Additionally, when both curves shift in the same direction (combinations B and H), the new equilibrium quantity will follow; however, the new equilibrium price is indeterminate. So, when both the demand and supply curves increase, the new equilibrium quantity increases but the new equilibrium price is indeterminate. And when both the demand and supply curves decrease, the new equilibrium quantity decreases; but the new equilibrium price is indeterminate.

Lastly, when both curves shift but in opposite directions (combinations C and G), the new equilibrium price follows in the same direction as the demand curve; however, the new equilibrium quantity is indeterminate. So, when the demand curve increases but the supply curve decreases, the new equilibrium price increases; however, the new equilibrium quantity is indeterminate. And when the demand curve decreases but the supply curve increases, the new equilibrium price decreases; however, the new equilibrium quantity is indeterminate.

CAUSES OF P & Q INDETERMINACY:

But what does "indeterminate" (in referring to fig. 7) mean? Why is the new market equilibrium price or quantity indeterminate? What does this indeterminacy depend upon?

"Indeterminate" refers to the fact that just by drawing the new curves, we cannot state with certainty whether the new market equilibrium price or quantity will increase, decrease, or stay the same. The answer depends upon the magnitude of their relative changes (i.e., demand and supply). Take figure 7, combination B, as an example: if both the demand and supply curves increase by the same magnitude, then the new equilibrium price stays the same. But if the demand curve increases by a greater magnitude than that of the supply curve, then the new equilibrium market price increases. Lastly, if the demand curve increases by a magnitude less than that of the supply curve, then the new equilibrium market price decreases. (You may want to draw these graphs to prove the directions of the new market equilibrium prices.) Without knowing the relative increase/decrease of both the demand and supply curves, we cannot state with certainty what will happen to the new market equilibrium price; ergo, we use the term "indeterminate".

Why is this important to know? While you may not be able to control the market demand curve (if you are a consumer) or the market supply curve (unless you are the sole producer), if changes occur to just the demand or the supply curve, you may be able to forecast its impact. However, when both curves change, the effect on the market is more difficult to forecast!

TESTING YOUR KNOWLEDGE *(I.E., YOUR ACQUIRED HUMAN CAPITAL)*

Determine whether the following statements are true or false. If false, can you explain why?

1. Together, a home theater system and an HD television are considered an example of complimentary goods.
2. A reduction in taxes will result in an increased supply curve; the supply curve will shift to the right.
3. An increase in the number of buyers in the market for 3-D TVs would cause the market demand curve for 3-D TVs to increase; the curve would shift to the right.
4. Assume there is a simultaneous increase in home foreclosures and decrease in consumer incomes. Based on this information, we can conclude with certainty that in the market for (non-newly built) single-family homes, the equilibrium price will decrease.
5. Assume the cost of certain inputs used to produce artificial Christmas trees (normal goods) increases and, at the same time, the economy moves into a recession, causing the incomes of consumers to decrease. As a result, the equilibrium quantity will decrease; but the equilibrium price cannot be determined.

Chapter 5. Market Disruptions

There is a lot of talk about "market disruptions" in the news these days. Terms such as "disruption innovations," "digital disruption," and "disruption in technology" are becoming commonplace themes. But what is a disruption, and how does it affect the market in which it occurs?

A "disruption" is anything that alters the natural function of market equilibrium. Examples include rent control/stabilization policies, changes in minimum wages, policies for free college education, stricter (or looser) policies on gas emissions, and more. All these disruptors will prevent the markets from freely functioning and arriving at its natural market equilibrium. Okay, you may state, so is that a good or a bad thing? We will discuss the impact of market disruptions (or interventions) and their effects under two scenarios, (1) when the disruption causes the equilibrium price to be set above the natural market equilibrium, and (2) when the disruption causes the equilibrium price to be set below the natural market equilibrium.

Disruptions Set above the Natural Market Equilibrium:

If we looked at a disruption where the price is set above the natural market equilibrium, the graph would look something like figure 1. In economic terms, a price set above the market equilibrium is called a "price floor"—the minimal price to be paid. So what policy interventions would cause a market price to be set above the natural market equilibrium?

PRICE FLOOR EXAMPLE & IMPLICATIONS:

One example would be the government setting a higher minimum wage rate. In the United States, according to the Department of Labor, there is a mandated minimum wage rate—the dollar amount an employee receives per hour of work—set at the federal level; there can be a different minimum wage rate set at the state and sometimes local levels.[18] Effective December 31, 2017, the federal minimum wage rate is $7.25 per hour. New York State's minimum wage rate is $10.40; meanwhile, New York City's minimum rate is $12.00 for firms with 10 or fewer employees—and $13.00 for firms with 11 or more employees. Effective December 31, 2018, these rates increased to $11.10, $13.50, and $15.00, respectfully.[19] Can you guess why the minimum wage rate is different at the federal, state, and local levels? (*Hint: were you thinking of "the cost of living"?*)

Assuming the 2017 wage rates, let's assume that the market for minimum-wage earners in New York City has adjusted to the natural equilibrium price of $13.00 for firms with 11 or more employees (see fig. 1, point C). At this equilibrium, both the quantity supplied of these workers and the quantity demanded for these workers is in equilibrium as well.

But what will happen with the wage rate increases in 2019, when the employers must pay these same workers $15 an hour for the same type of work? While these firms will have no choice but to adhere to this "disruption," what will be its effect? Graphically, we can see that this new price, set above the natural market equilibrium condition, intersects the demand curve at point A and the supply curve at point B. Thus, the quantity supplied (i.e., employees willing to work at $15 an hour) is much greater than the quantity demanded (i.e., employers willing to pay their workers the

---

18 Wage and Hour Division, 2017.

19 Minimum Wage, 2017.

increased hourly wage of $15). This, in all likelihood, will cause a "surplus" of employees in the market that want to work at the increased minimum wage rate (i.e., the new price) of $15 an hour. Numerically, this surplus can be calculated by the difference between the quantity supplied and quantity demanded of workers. As an example, if at point A (fig. 1), the quantity demanded (Qd) equaled 52,000 employers willing to hire workers at the new higher wage rate of $15 per hour. However, at point B, the quantity supplied (Qs) equaled 69,500 workers that were available and available and willing to work for $15 an hour. Thus, the surplus of workers would equal Qs – Qd = 69,500 – 52,000 = 16,500.

Figure 1. Disruption set above natural market equilibrium-price floor

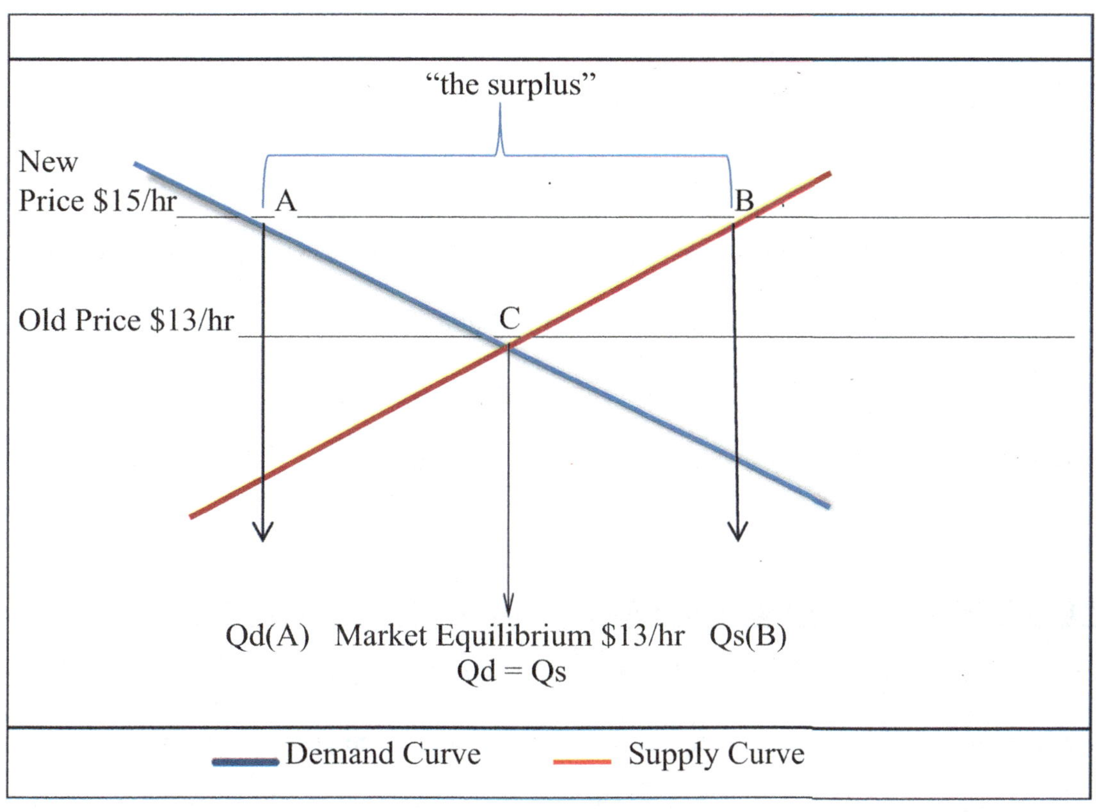

In reality, when the price of wages rises, there is a reduction in employment opportunities for low-wage earners—possibly leading to a higher rate of unemployment for this classification of workers. Reduced employment occurs as employers, faced with paying higher hourly wages, may decide to save money by consolidating their workflow and laying off employees.

For smaller firms such as neighborhood "mom-and-pop" stores, an increase in the minimum wage rate may possibly result in a larger underground economy (i.e., workers being paid "off-the-books"). In this case, employees may accept lower hourly wages as they may not report (and thus not pay income taxes on) some or all of their wages to the Internal Revenue Service. While being paid off-the-books may sound appealing to some employees and employers, we will take a more in-depth look at its negative impact on the economy as a whole when we discuss macroeconomic policies and growth.[20]

So, in this scenario, the government's intention to increase minimum wages is admirable, and minimum-wage earners are the beneficiaries of the policy. However, *ceteris paribus*, higher costs for firms may cause unfavorable consequences (such as decreases in product quality and/or quantity, higher consumer prices, and layoffs). Similar analysis, as in the example of an increase in the wage rate, can be applied to all market interventions where prices are set above the natural equilibrium market price (i.e., price floor).

DISRUPTIONS SET BELOW THE NATURAL MARKET EQUILIBRIUM:

If we looked at a disruption that is set below the natural market equilibrium, the graph would look something like figure 2. In economic terms, a price set below the market equilibrium is called a "price ceiling"—the maximum price to be paid.

---

[20] For those of you who are interested in the ramifications of being paid off-the-books from both the employer and employee perspectives, I invite you to read the article by Marz, 2018, *"Can I Get Into Trouble if My Employer Pays Me Under the Table?"*

PRICE CEILING EXAMPLES & IMPLICATIONS:

So what policy interventions would cause the price in a market to be set below the natural market equilibrium? Examples include usury laws (i.e., state statutes) that stipulate the maximum interest rates that can be imposed on loans; President Nixon's 1971 cap on gas prices; the 2008 food price ceilings imposed by the government of Venezuela; and State Farm's 2009 cap on property insurance rates as a result of hurricanes in Florida.[21]

A further example of a price ceiling would be the classic textbook illustration of rent-controlled apartments. After World War II, the US government wanted to make housing affordable, so many cities adopted rent-control legislature. Rent control was a city mandate placing a maximum amount of monthly rent (i.e., price ceiling) a landlord could charge for an apartment.

In looking at figure 2, we use the government-mandated rent-control legislature to examine the disruption to the housing market. Without rent control, the equilibrium price for a given apartment is at point C. For apartments that fall under rent-control guidelines, the new price—the price ceiling—is set below the market equilibrium. This will cause the quantity demanded of rent-controlled apartments (at point B) to be greater than the quantity supplied (at point A).

[21]State Farm to stop insuring Florida, 2009.

Figure 2. Disruption set below natural market equilibrium-price ceiling

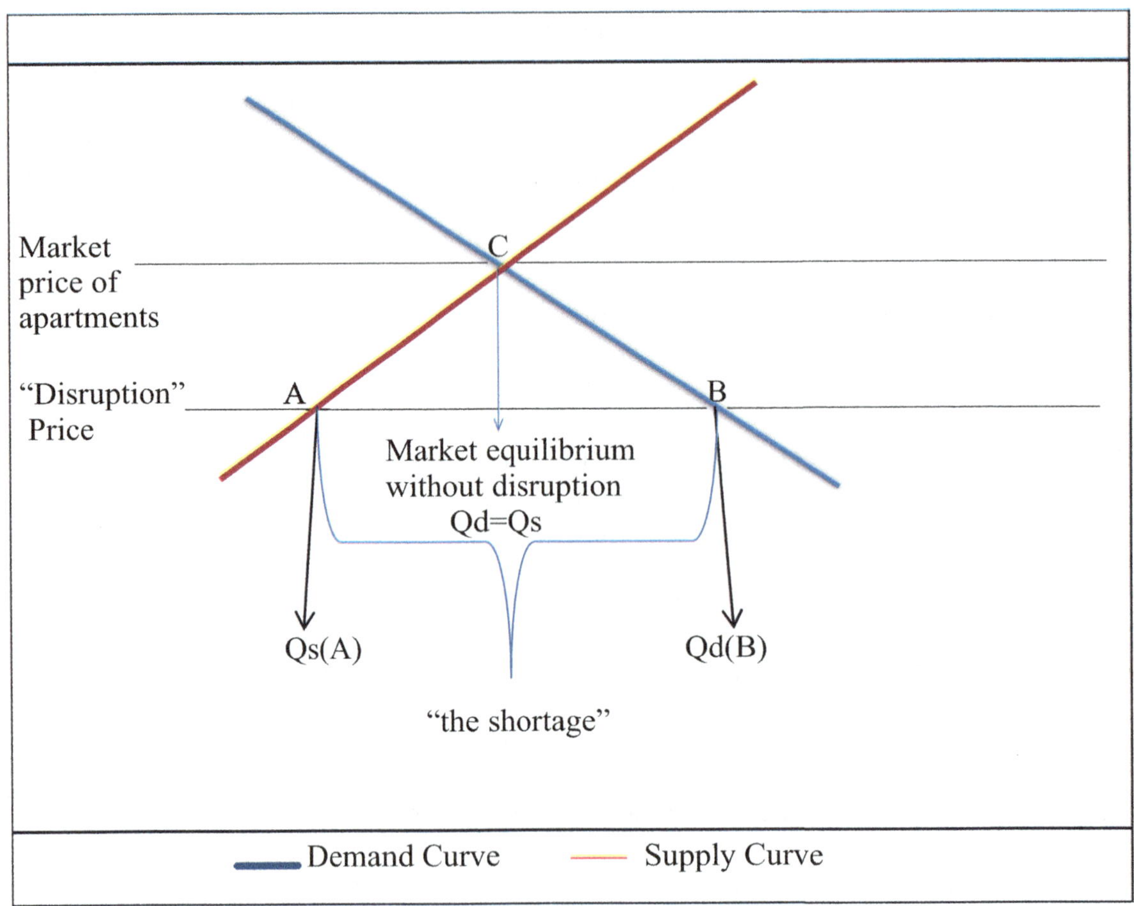

In contrast to a price floor, under a price ceiling condition, the quantity demanded [point Qd(B)] is greater than the quantity supplied [point Qs(A)], causing a shortage of rent-controlled apartments. Numerically, this shortage can be calculated as the difference between the quantity demanded and quantity supplied. As an example, if (at point B) the quantity demanded (Qd) equaled 93,000 rental units and (at point A) the quantity supplied (Qs) equaled 79,000, then the shortage of rent-controlled apartments would equal Qd – Qs = 93,000 – 79,000 = 14,000.

So, the tenants of the rent-controlled apartment are the beneficiaries, while the landlords lose out in earning additional rental incomes. In addition, how likely do you think the landlords of rent-controlled apartments are to upkeep and make quick repairs on these apartments? Not very likely or quickly! In fact, in a poll of 464 economists taken in 1990, most agreed that rent control reduces both the quantity and quality of available housing.[22]

So, while the government's intention to keep rent-controlled apartment prices low (below the natural market equilibrium) is admirable, and tenants of rent-controlled apartments are beneficiaries of the policy, unfavorable consequences (such as apartment shortages, decreased apartment quality, and lower rental incomes for landlords) also arise. Similar analysis, as in the example of a decrease in the monthly rental price of rent-control apartments, can be applied to all market interventions where prices are set below the equilibrium market price (i.e., price ceiling).

In sum, disruptions (i.e., price ceilings and price floors) to a market's natural equilibrium cause that market to function inefficiently. Though some economic participants benefit from these disruptions, they may also cause negative repercussions in the economy.

[22] Alson, Kearl, & Vaughan (1992).

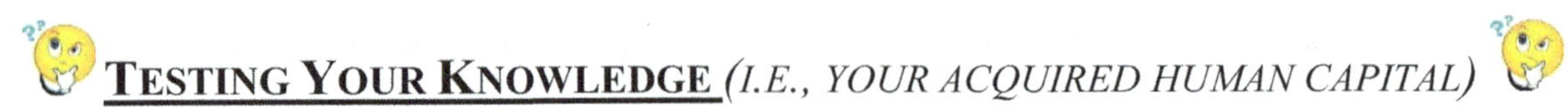

TESTING YOUR KNOWLEDGE *(I.E., YOUR ACQUIRED HUMAN CAPITAL)*

Determine whether the following statements are true or false. If false, can you explain why?

1. An example of government-caused market disruption is price ceiling—where a price is placed above the natural market equilibrium.
2. Price ceilings cause market surpluses.
3. The condition where prices are set below the equilibrium market price is referred to as a "price floor."
4. When a disruption in price is set above the natural market equilibrium, the quantity demanded will be greater than the quantity supplied.
5. Government interventions causing disruption on the free market equilibrium poses no negative effects on the economy.

CHAPTER 6. BUSINESS STRUCTURES & EFFECT ON MARKET EQUILIBRIUM

In previous chapters, we have seen how the market equilibrium is affected by the determinants of demand, the determinants of supply, and market disruptions. We will now turn our attention to four different business structures—pure/perfect competition, monopolistic competition, oligopoly, and monopoly—and see how each structure affects the markets in which it serves.

PURE OR PERFECT COMPETITION:

A purely competitive industry is usually characterized by very many buyers and sellers wanting and selling the same (i.e., homogeneous) quality of products. Examples of pure competitive businesses are neighborhood delis or bodegas, dollar stores, and local real estate offices. However, for perfect competition to exist, other characteristics from both the buyer and seller must be met. Some of these characteristics and assumptions are listed below:

1. A firm's primary goal is to **maximize profits**.
2. In the long run, firms will make **"normal" profits**—a condition where economic profits are equal to zero.

   We define **economic profits** (EP) as the difference between total revenues (TR) minus total economic costs (TEC); or, EP = TR - TEC,

   Where, **revenue** = price × quantity

   economic costs = explicit costs + implicit costs

   explicit costs are all costs directly associated with the running of a firm, such as employee wages, rent, insurance premiums, advertising, etc.

implicit costs, or opportunity costs, are the costs associated with the value of the "next best alternative", such as the forfeited salary the owner earned when s/he was working for a company.[23]

So, in a perfectly competitive industry, economic profits are equal to zero—does this mean that a business is not "profitable" in the traditional sense of the word? Does it mean that the store owner is working in the business without drawing down income/wages? The answer is NO! Owners' wages are "captured" (or are included in the calculations) under explicit costs, and the wages s/he would have earned if s/he were working for another company are "captured" (or are included in the calculations) under implicit costs!

3. Firms have **perfect or full information** about the product or service it produces/sells.
4. Firms have **legal rights to own and buy** product/property.
5. There are **no barriers to enter or exit the market**. Examples may include: administrative, legal, background & financial disclosure obstacles. So, liquor stores are not an example of "perfect competition" as the owners of these establishments must obtain a liquor license, undergo background checks, etc.; all obstacles in entering the market.
6. **Perfect factor mobility** exists in this market, where factor mobility refers to the interchange of land, labor, and capital in the production of final goods and services. For example, the same employee has the skills for working in both the Accounts Receivable and Accounts Payable departments. This factor mobility is effective in making long-term adjustments when changes in market conditions occur.

---

[23] The difference between explicit and implicit/opportunity costs can best be explained as follows: When asked, "how much did your college education cost?", most students would spew the total dollar amount of tuition. Some would add tuition plus the cost of books, supplies, room and board, and/or transportation. All of these costs are "explicit" costs. The implicit/opportunity cost of your education is the foregone salary you could have been earning if you were working full time and not in school.

7. **No externalities** exist in this market, where externalities refer to the costs or benefits of an economic activity that does not affect third parties (i.e., noneconomic participants).

   An example of a positive externality (i.e., benefit) is finding a medicine to cure an infectious disease. The direct participants in this economic activity are the suppliers of the medicine who sell it to the consumers who need and buy it. The positive externality is associated with the fact that this economic activity positively affects other parties—all those that would have contracted the infectious disease if they had not been treated.

   An example of a negative externality (i.e., cost) is pollution. Say a firm engages in the production of a product that consumers want and buy. However, the production of this product causes pollution. Pollution affects all the surrounding people that are near the production site (i.e., third parties); thus, it is a negative externality.
8. **No transaction costs** exists in this market. This means that buyers and sellers do not incur costs in buying or selling a product, such as costs associated with making a financial trade or buying a property.
9. **No network effects** exist in this market; where the "network effects" refer to the perceived indirect value (of a good or service) that is gained as more people use the network. In a pure competitive market, "networks" will deter the entrance of new firms entering the industry as they do not have an "established" network and no "perceived added value"! So, Gmail and T-Mobile are not an example of "perfect competition" as their businesses are highly network dependent.

Please note that in a purely competitive market, no one participant has the power to set prices, so every participant is a price-taker. Why would this be? Imagine that you, as a buyer, have just come home from grocery shopping. While putting your grocery items away, you notice that you forgot to buy milk. So, once again, you leave your home to purchase a quart of milk. As you only want to purchase one item, you decide to simply walk to one of your local neighborhood stores. Now, what if the neighborhood stores have different prices for a quart of milk? Even if you are initially unaware of the differing prices, given time, you will become aware of this information and only buy milk from the neighborhood store that had the lowest price. All rational consumers in your neighborhood will follow suit; as a result, no (or almost no) milk will be purchased from the other local stores with higher milk prices! But neighborhood stores will not want to carry milk if it does not sell. Therefore, knowing that many local stores carry milk, the neighborhood stores will set their milk prices at the market equilibrium price.

Now you may ask, why wouldn't a store sell the quart of milk at a lower price—lower than the other neighborhood stores? While one local store may advertise a sale on milk (a short-term marketing technique used to attract people to the store in the hope that they will purchase other items), its owners may cite a few reasons why they would not price the milk below market equilibrium (a long-term lowering of the price of milk in relation to other neighborhood stores carrying milk). Some reasons may include milk is just one of many products of convenience they carry, or they do not want to engage in a price war.[24] But, ultimately, the answer is the store would not maximize its profits if it was to lower the price of milk!

In sum, if you are an entrepreneur or the manager of a purely competitive firm (a price-taker), the only way to increase long-term profits [where economic profits = revenue (price × quantity) – economic costs] is to (1) increase the quantity of products/services sold (only possible if your market competition decreases or if your number of buyers increase) and/or (2) cut costs.

---

[24] In economics, the concept of "price wars" is fully explored in the field of game theory.

MONOPOLISTIC COMPETITION:

A monopolistic competitive industry is usually characterized by very many buyers and sellers wanting and selling, respectively, products of homogeneous (but not identical) quality. Examples of monopolistic competitive businesses include salons/barbershops, restaurants, and clothing stores.

For monopolistic competition to exist, other characteristics from both the buyer and seller must be met. Some of these characteristics and assumptions are listed below:

1. Once again, the firm's primary goal is to **maximize profits.**
2. In the **short run**, firms will **make positive economic profits** [where revenues > economic (explicit + implicit) costs]. But new firms will see these positive economic profits and enter the market; so, in the long run, economic profits will be equal to zero—the same condition as in a perfect competitive market structure.
3. **Imperfect or incomplete information** of product or service exists in this market. For example, if you want a professional massage, you can search prices, services offered, and customer reviews of all neighboring massage salons. Even once inside a salon, you can look at all the listed services and prices, as well as view customers' facial/body expressions as they are leaving to gauge their levels of satisfaction. However, you will not be able to acquire the full knowledge of how well the masseuse/masseur massages until after s/he has given you a massage!
4. **Legal rights to own and buy** product/property exists in this market.
5. There are **no barriers to enter or exit** the market.

PRODUCT DIFFERENTIATION & ITS IMPORTANCE:

In addition to the previous listed characteristics, the main feature of monopolistic competition is that products are differentiated. There are four types of differentiation:

1. ***Physical product differentiation***, where firms use size, design, color, shape, performance, and other features to make their products different.
2. ***Marketing differentiation***, where firms use distinctive packaging, celebrity sponsorships/endorsements, and other promotional techniques to distinguish their products/services.
3. ***Human capital differentiation***, where firms create differences through the skills, levels of training received, distinctive dress codes, etc., of its employees.
4. ***Distribution differentiation***, where firms create differences via their distribution channels: mail order, phone, television, Internet, auto-replenishing orders, etc.

The ability to differentiate a product or product line enables firms to do the following:

1. Create brand or firm loyalty
2. Engage in advertising (which leads to increased costs) in order to publicize this differentiation of products or services
3. Set their own prices—firms are now price-makers (as opposed to purely competitive markets, where firms are price-takers)
4. Make independent decisions about price and output (given their ability to differentiate products and their costs of production)
5. Have a more significant role in the management of their business due to the increased risks associated with product differentiation decision-making

In sum, if you are an entrepreneur or the manager of a monopolistic competitive firm (a price-maker), you may increase profits by (1) increasing your prices (provided you have differentiated your product to be perceived as a higher-quality product) and/or (2) increasing your quantities sold (by creating a need for this niche product). However, costs may be more difficult to decrease.

OLIGOPOLY:

An oligopolistic industry is usually characterized by very many buyers and a few sellers wanting and selling, respectively, products of homogeneous (but not identical) quality. When a market is comprised of only a few major firms, it is said to be highly concentrated. And although only a few firms dominate the market, it is also possible that smaller firms can create a niche (for example, Sun Country Airlines or Spirit Airlines). Examples of oligopolistic businesses include those in the airline, oil, and gas industries.

For oligopolies to exist, other characteristics from both the buyer and seller must be met. Some of these characteristics, and assumptions made of the market participants are listed below:

1. There exists a **great amount of interdependence** among the firms. In a market with few sellers, when one firm changes price or alters its quantity produced, it directly affects the other firms in the industry. Therefore, under an oligopoly market structure, a firm must not only consider the market demand for its product but also the reactions of other firms in the industry.
2. Similar to monopolistic competition (and as opposed to pure competition and monopoly), oligopolies must **engage in aggressive advertising**/sales promotions (which leads to increased costs) in order to gain market shares and maximize revenues.

3. Unlike the other three market structures, oligopolies **face indeterminate demand curves**. Each firm cannot predict the consequence of its price–output decisions; if it makes a change in price, it cannot assume rivals will keep their own prices unchanged. (See the duopoly scenario discussion of Jesse & Taylor's demand schedule below.)
4. **Legal rights to own and buy** product/property exist in this market.
5. There are **no barriers to enter or exit** the market; but in the long run, high capital requirements, exclusive patents/licenses, or controls over specialized inputs may make it difficult for new firms to enter this industry.
6. **Prices are rigid**. We say prices are "rigid" because if any firm decides to cut prices, the rival firms will follow suit, leading to a "price war."[25] However, the opposite is not true. If any firm decides to increase prices to increase profits, rival firms may not follow suit.
7. **Strategic thinking is required** from the entrepreneur or manager of an oligopolistic firm. This is because, in order to find the general equilibrium, game theory strategies will need to be employed. (See Duopoly Scenario-Nash Equilibrium.)

In sum, under perfect competition, monopolistic competition, and monopoly, sellers do not have to worry about how their rivals will react because either the sellers are small in comparison to the market or the seller is the monopolist. However, under an oligopolistic market, a firm is big enough to affect the market. As there are only a few firms in the industry, each firm must respond to its rivals' choices about price and output. Therefore, a dilemma is created—a firm must choose between cooperating with rivals or following its own self-interest.

---

[25] Over the years, the airline industry has been notorious for its price wars; and Amazon and Walmart have been engaged in a price war since early 2017.

As an example, if all the producers of oil got together (i.e., formed a cartel) and decided (i.e., colluded) to limit their output/distribution of oil, the price of oil would increase. However, each oil producer has self-interest as an incentive to expand its output and thus increase revenue! So, what should an oligopolistic firm do? The techniques of game theory are used to solve for the equilibrium condition in an oligopoly market structure.

DUOPOLY SCENARIO-PRISONER'S DILEMMA:

A duopoly is a form of oligopoly. It is defined as two firms that dominate the market, whereby each firm is forced to anticipate and carefully consider its rival's reactions to business decisions. Table 1 represents a classic game theory example of duopoly—the prisoner's dilemma. In this scenario, Bonnie and Clyde have been arrested and are in separate holding rooms at the police station. The police do not have enough evidence to charge them, and the prisoners' only hope is for none of them to confess to the crime. Each prisoner is given the same offer by the arresting officer: "rat out" your partner and you will be given a lighter sentence; however, you must confess to the crime BEFORE your partner does.

We can summarize the dilemma's outcomes in the following table:

Table 1. Prisoner's dilemma outcomes

		Bonnie	
		Do not talk	Talk
Clyde	Do not talk	(Free, free)	(Guilty, light sentence)
	Talk	(Light sentence, guilty)	(Guilty, guilty)

Faced with this dilemma, Clyde reviews the outcome options:

- If Clyde decides to not talk, he will either be set free (if Bonnie also decides to not talk) or found guilty (if Bonnie decides to talk).
- If Clyde decides to talk, he will either be offered a lighter sentence (if Bonnie decides to not talk) or found guilty (if Bonnie also decides to talk).

Bonnie also reviews her outcome options:

- If Bonnie decides to not talk, she will either be set free (if Clyde also decides not to talk) or found guilty (if Clyde decides to talk).
- If Bonnie decides to talk, she will either be offered a lighter sentence (if Clyde decides to not talk) or found guilty (if Clyde also decides to talk).

In both their cases, each is better off if they decide not to talk; thus, the police, without having enough evidence to convict them, will set both free. This would be the optimal solution to the dilemma. However, is Bonnie sure that Clyde will not confess? Is Clyde sure that Bonnie will not confess? Faced with this uncertainty, and being unable to collude, they both choose to talk in hopes of receiving the lighter sentence! Naturally, as they both talk, this leads to a verdict of guilty for both—the suboptimal solution.

Let's extend this example to a case of two firms in a market.

Duopoly Scenario-Nash Equilibrium:

We will analyze the payoff matrix in the following fictitious duopoly situation, where Jesse and Taylor are the only two producers of large sunflowers in their township. To simplify the exercise, we assume zero costs in production and that both Jesse and Taylor are rational decision makers. The market demand schedule-the quantity and price columns in Table 2-gives us the total quantity (total combined output for Jesse and Taylor) of sunflowers that consumers are willing to buy (on a weekly basis) at a given price. Example, at a price of 50¢, consumers are willing to purchase 1,000 large sunflowers.

Table 2. Market demand & total revenue

Quantity (Q) of Large Sunflowers per Week	Price (P) per Sunflower	Total Revenue (P × Q) per Week
1,100	$0.00	$0
1,050	$0.20	$263
1,000	$0.50	$500
950	$0.75	$713
900	$1.00	$900
850	$1.25	$1,063
800	$1.50	$1,200
750	$1.75	$1,313
700	$2.00	$1,400
650	$2.25	$1,463
600	$2.50	$1,500
550	$2.75	$1,513
500	$3.00	$1,500
450	$3.25	$1,463
400	$3.50	$1,140
350	$3.75	$1,313
300	$4.00	$1,200
250	$4.25	$1,063
200	$4.50	$900
150	$4.75	$713
100	$5.00	$500
50	$5.25	$263
0	$5.50	$0

Faced with the market demand for large sunflowers per week, Jesse and Taylor calculate the total revenue for each of the combinations of price and quantity—as seen in the last column in Table 2.

Jesse and Taylor, as they are the only two suppliers in the industry, face the following dilemma—should they collude, or should they follow their self-interest and try to gain market share?

If Jesse and Taylor were to collude, they would each produce 500 large sunflowers per week, sell them at $3 per flower, and make $1,500 in revenues per week. Why would they agree on this price and quantity? Note that a quantity of 600 would also yield $1,500 in revenues, but the total quantity supplied of 1,200 (each producing 600 sunflowers) would surpass the maximum quantity demanded in the market. Similarly, if each produced at a quantity of 550, they would make a greater amount of total revenues per week ($1,513); however, the total quantity supplied (1,100) would surpass the maximum quantity demanded in the market at positive prices. (As seen in Table 2, the maximum market quantity demanded given positive prices is 1,050 sunflowers per week.)

But is the collusion sustainable? After all, both Jesse and Taylor want to maximize profits—and they can see that total weekly revenues are highest ($1,513) at a quantity of 550 sunflowers and a unit price of $2.75. So, what if one of them decides to "break" the collusive understanding to follow his self-interest and earn higher revenues?

Following the self-interest strategy, Jesse would choose to produce 550 sunflowers per week at a unit price of $2.75; this would yield total weekly revenues of $1,513 (the maximum weekly profits given the demand). If Jesse committed to this price–output decision, it would leave Taylor to supply the rest of the large sunflowers—a quantity of 500 (i.e., the maximum market demand of

1,050 large sunflowers – the 550 large sunflowers supplied by Jesse) at the same price of $2.75. This would yield Taylor total weekly revenues of $1,375—lower weekly revenues than those earned by Jesse's price–output strategy.

And if Taylor followed his self-interest, the same choices (i.e., the choices made by Jesse) would be made. As a result, Jesse would be the one earning less total weekly revenues!

However, if they were to decide to share the market equally, each would produce 525[26] sunflowers per week at a unit price of $2.75 (the price where total revenue was at its highest). Then each of them would earn total weekly revenues of $1,443.75 (i.e., 525 × $2.75 = $1,443.75).

So, what is the equilibrium condition for this duopoly? We can write out the payoff options in a 2x2 matrix format—Jesse's and Taylor's total revenues should they choose to stick with the collusion strategy, or should they choose not to collude.

Table 3. Payoff schedule

		Taylor	
		Collude	Do not collude
Jesse	Collude	($1,500, $1,500)	($1,375, $1,513)
	Do not collude	($1,513, $1,375)	($1,443.75, $1,443.75)

[26] 525 units of sunflowers are derived from the total quantity demanded of 1050 (at positive prices) divided equally by Jesse & Taylor (i.e., 1050 / 2 = 525).

Faced with these price–output decisions, Jesse reviews his payoff options:

- If Jesse decides to collude, he can either earn $1,500 (if Taylor also decides to collude) or earn $1,375 (if Taylor decides not to collude).
- If Jesse decides not to collude, he can either earn $1,513 (if Taylor decides to collude) or earn $1,443.75 (if Taylor also decides not to collude).

Taylor also reviews his options:

- If Taylor decides to collude, he can either earn $1,500 (if Jesse also decides to collude) or earn $1,375 (if Jesse decides not to collude).
- If Taylor decides not to collude, he can either earn $1,513 (if Jesse decides to collude) or earn $1,443.75 (if Jesse also decides not to collude).

In both their cases, making independent decisions, each is better off if they decide not to collude. In review of each of the possible payoff outcomes in Table 3, earnings of $1,513 are greater than earning of $1,500; and earnings of $1,443.75 are greater than earnings of $1,375. As a result, both Jesse and Taylor decide not to collude. However, jointly, when both make the decision of not colluding, this means each will produce and supply 525 large sunflowers per week at a price of $2.75, each earning total weekly revenues of $1,443.75—highlighted quadrant 4 in Table 3. Therefore, "do not collude" is the dominant strategy for either firm, independent of the other firm's strategy, and gives the highest payoff for both.[27] This equilibrium condition in a duopoly is referred as the "**Cournot-Nash equilibrium**".[28]

For "general" games in an oligopoly market structure, a Nash equilibrium may be defined as a combination of strategies (one for each firm) in which no firm—given the strategies chosen by the

---

[27] This game theory decision is referred to as "joint rationality"; each player is best responding to the other player.

[28] I would like to thank my colleague Dr. Utteeyo Dasgupta for his review of the duopoly payoff matrix explanations.

rival oligopoly firm(s)—has an alternative strategy that yields a higher payoff. Therefore, once a price-output equilibrium is found, no firm has an incentive to alter his/her strategy.

In sum, if you are an entrepreneur or the manager of an oligopolistic firm (a price-maker), faced with "rigid" prices, you will have to react to the response of your rival(s) to reach a price–output equilibrium. Thus, the only way to increase profits is to (1) increase the quantity sold (only possible if your market competition decreases or if your number of buyers increase) and/or (2) cut costs.

MONOPOLY & WHY GOVERNMENT REGULATES:

A monopoly is characterized by very many buyers and only one seller wanting and selling, respectively, a product. Although only one firm dominates the market, it is also possible that a few smaller firms can create a niche in this market.

Privately held monopolies in the United States are illegal (as per the Sherman Antitrust Act of 1890 and the Clayton Antitrust Act of 1914). However, due to high economies of scale, firms within some industries are more prone to form "natural" monopolies. Examples include the water, electricity, and gas industries. As it is in the economy's best interest to discourage competition for these natural monopolies, the government has created regulatory bodies to prevent the abuse of monopoly power. As an example, the United States Commission's Bureau of Competition adjudicates cases where a merger may capture more than 25% of market share. The commission decides whether to allow or block the merger.

Thus, the government regulates monopolies for three main reasons:

1. To protect consumers from having a monopolist set high prices
2. To protect other businesses from having a monopolist corner a market
3. To protect the quality of service from having a monopolist evade a minimum standard of service

In sum, if you are an entrepreneur or the manager of a regulated monopoly (a price-maker), you may be less concerned about decreasing costs. But you may increase profits by petitioning the government for an increase in prices. (This naturally assumes you can substantiate the reason for the price increase.) However, please note that you cannot affect quantity as you are the sole supplier in the market!

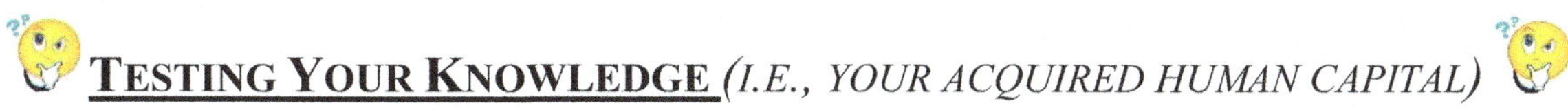

TESTING YOUR KNOWLEDGE *(I.E., YOUR ACQUIRED HUMAN CAPITAL)*

Determine whether the following statements are true or false. If false, can you explain why?

1. In perfect competitive markets, sellers are price-takers.
2. Implicit costs are associated with opportunity costs, the value/costs of the next best alternative.
3. The market structure categorized by many buyers and firms selling homogeneous (but not identical) products is called "monopolistic competition."
4. Game theory is best used under an oligopoly market structure to determine the dominant price–output strategy.
5. The government regulates natural monopolies to protect the interests of both consumers and producers.

PART III. UNDERSTANDING MACROECONOMICS

CHAPTER 7.
UNDERSTANDING NATIONAL INCOME

CHAPTER 8.
FOREIGN EXCHANGE RATES

CHAPTER 9.
UNEMPLOYMENT *VS.* INFLATION, DEFLATION & ECONOMIC INDICATORS

CHAPTER 10.
MONEY & BANKING

CHAPTER 11.
MONETARY & FISCAL POLICY

CHAPTER 7. UNDERSTANDING NATIONAL INCOME

Macroeconomics is the study of the economy as a whole. In this world of connectivity, where information is readily available by anyone who has access to the Internet, we have a growing number of multinational businesses as well as many individuals privately selling their products and services abroad. We need to have a better understanding of both (1) how the economy functions in our own country, state, and city and (2) how our policies affect (and are affected by) the policies of other countries.

While there are many topics that fall under the purview of macroeconomics, the remainder of this book will explore the following: economic growth, national income, consumption, savings, investments, government spending, net export spending, restrictions to trade, currency & exchange rate regimes, unemployment, inflation, economic indicators, money & banking, the Federal Reserve, monetary policies, interest rates, fiscal policies, balanced budgets, and economic equilibrium.

GNP VS. GDP:

When we speak about economic growth, we have to ask, "How do we measure the income of an economy over time?" In defining our nation's income, we must first distinguish between the terms "Gross National Products (GNP)" and "Gross Domestic Products (GDP)."

GNP is defined as "the total value (in dollars) of all final goods and services produced by the country's nationals." As an example, GNP will include the dollar value of a US company's (i.e.,

McDonald's) final output in the United States as well as the dollar value of what it (McDonald's) produces outside of the United States (i.e., in Nicaragua, Peru, Italy, Morocco, Singapore, etc.).

In contrast, GDP is defined as "the total value (in dollars) of all final goods and services produced within a nation's borders." This includes spending from a country's nationals and non-nationals. As an example, GDP will include the dollar value of a US company's (i.e., General Motors) final output in the United States as well as the dollar value of a non-US-based company's final output (i.e., British-based Rolls-Royce manufacturing engine parts in Virginia, or German-based Siemens producing power-plant turbines in Charlotte, N.C.) that is doing business in the United States.

EXPENDITURE APPROACH TO GDP:

There are two mathematical approaches to calculating GDP—the income approach and the expenditure approach. As both approaches will yield the same total dollar value, this book will focus on the expenditure approach to GDP. The expenditure approach to GDP, while less mathematical in nature, is convenient as it allows us to determine which sector of the economy is contributing to the overall income of the nation (and by how much). Mathematically, it is simply the addition of four variables that represent different sectors of the economy:

$$Y = C + I + G + NE \tag{1.1}$$

where Y = GDP (total income for the nation)

C = consumption by individuals (the household sector of the economy)

I = investment spending by businesses (the business sector of the economy)

G = government spending (the government sector of the economy)

NE = net export spending (exports – imports; the foreign sector of the economy)

Before we discuss each of these four variables in further detail, we should first take note of what is excluded from the GDP calculation.

EXCLUSIONS TO GDP:

Because we do not want to "double count" (and thus overstate) the value of our nation's total (i.e., aggregate) spending, we only calculate the production of final goods and services; and, we do not count intermediate goods or services. For example, take the production of a car. The final good in this case is the car itself, so the dollar value of the car is included in GDP. However, its steering wheel, tires, seats, windshields, side-view mirrors, floor mats, motor, and battery are all intermediate goods—products used in the production of the final good. Their dollar values will not be included when calculating GDP. If we were to include the dollar value of these intermediate products, we would be double counting the total dollar value—as the price of the car already accounts for all the products used to manufacture the car!

In addition to intermediate goods, there are other exclusions in the calculation of GDP; they are:

- **Public transfer payments** are payments made to individuals or firms (in terms of subsidies) from the government for services previously performed. Examples include social security checks and veterans' benefits. The GDP does not include this income because it is not exchanged for new products.
- **Private transfer payments** are payments given to individuals or firms as a form of gift whereby no exchange of new production is required of the recipient in receipt of the payment. These may include monetary gifts to charitable organizations or to loved ones on birthdays, holidays, or special occasions.
- **Secondhand goods** are products that are resold (generally at a lower price); these

products are also referred to as "used," "gently used," "refurbished," and/or "previously owned." You can find and purchase secondhand goods from thrift shops (i.e., more notably the Salvation Army or Goodwill Industries), bookstores, used car dealerships, and more. The dollar values of these products are not added to the calculation of GDP because they were calculated when the products were first produced and sold.

- **Securities *(i.e., stocks, bonds, etc.)* & private investment *(i.e., capital buyouts)* transactions** are not included in GDP as the individual or firm is merely redistributing a money investment previously earned in the production of a good or service.
- **Legal & illegal underground activities** are not included in GDP. The term "underground" means that an economic activity is transacted but its dollar value is not reported to the Internal Revenue Service (IRS). Therefore, no taxes are assessed on the value of the good(s) or service(s) produced. However, we should distinguish whether that activity is legal or illegal. As an example, babysitting is a legal activity (i.e., there are no laws that state that a person cannot babysit in exchange for wages). There is also no law that states that a babysitter cannot be paid in cash. However, if the babysitter does not report this income to the IRS when filing taxes, it now becomes an "underground" (yet legal) economic transaction. By contrast, the production and distribution of nonmedicinal drugs (e.g., cocaine) by a private citizen is illegal. As such, private citizens distributing these drugs would not file taxes on the income earned. Thus, this transaction would be considered an "underground" (and illegal) economic activity. Having made the distinction between legal and illegal underground activities, please be aware that any earnings

not reported to the IRS (i.e., conducted in the "underground economy") are subject to legal ramifications.

The government and various research groups attempt to estimate the dollar value of the underground economy. However, whether the economic activity is legal or illegal, the fact remains that its dollar value is not reported to the IRS. As such, the dollar value from these activities are not included in the official calculation of a nation's GDP.

Having discussed how we measure a country's income, we will now discuss, in detail, the four components of the expenditure approach to calculating Gross Domestic Product.

CONSUMPTION:

Consumption is defined as "the total dollar value spent by the household sector of the economy." When consumption spending increases, GDP increases, and vice versa. This is why on Black Friday (or during the Christmas holidays) you hear the news discuss whether consumer spending is weak or strong. In fact, websites such as Statistic Brain report Black Friday's consumer spending by year and by top companies![29]

According to the World Bank, on average, the annual percentage worldwide growth of households' final consumption expenditure has been on the decline from 1971 to 2015.[30] However, this is not true for individualized countries.

---

[29] Statistic Brain, 2016.

[30] Household final consumption expenditure (annual % growth), 2017.

Spenders *vs.* Savers Countries:

In fact, countries may be categorized as "spenders" or "savers." The World Bank reports the ranking of 186 countries by the annual percentage of household consumption per capita[31], where "rank #1" refers to the biggest spender country (highest per capita annual percentage of household consumption) and "rank #186" refers to the biggest saver country (lowest per capita annual percentage of household consumption).

As of 2015, the top five saver countries are the Russian Federation (ranking #182), Antigua & Barbuda (#183), the United Arab Emirates (#184), Zimbabwe (#185), and Ukraine (#186). Other high saver countries of interest are Switzerland (#140), Jamaica (#158), Japan (#164), and Brazil (#175).

On the other hand, the top five spender countries or territories are Côte d'Ivoire, Liberia, West Bank and Gaza, Uganda, and Trinidad & Tobago (ranking #1 through #5, respectively). Another high spender country of interest is China, which is ranked at #9.

Countries falling in the middle of the ranking include the United States (#72), Mexico (#87), Italy (#97), the United Kingdom (#101), France (#115), and Canada (#116).[32] However, please note that if we were to divide the rankings in half (i.e., spenders versus savers), the United States would be

---

[31] Final consumption expenditure (% of GDP), formerly "total consumption," is the sum of final household consumption expenditure (private consumption) and general final government consumption expenditure (general government consumption). This estimate includes any statistical discrepancy in the use of resources relative to the supply of resources.

[32] Household final consumption expenditure per capita growth (annual %), 2017.

considered a spender country. This would explain why the United States pays special attention to and closely tracks consumption spending!

So, where does consumption spending (or saving) come from? At the consumer level, if we were to look at an individual's yearly income stream, in its simplest form, we could calculate the net or disposable income as follows:

Net/disposable income = gross income – deductions – taxes

Where, **Gross income** is income received from all non-exclusionary income streams, such as salaries, wages, tips, capital gains, dividends, interest, rent payments, pensions, and alimony.

Deductions are subtractions from income to include all government allowable non-taxable deductions from income. These deductions include the dollar value of contributions to individual retirement accounts, health care flexible spending accounts, and transit commuter benefit programs.[33]

Taxes are subtractions from income that are requested by (and paid to) the government, such as federal, state, and city taxes; social security; and Medicare.

Individual consumers can either save or spend their net disposable incomes. Figure 1 diagrams the flow of an individual's net disposable income.

[33] As these allowable deductions are set by the government, these deductions and/or the maximum dollar value that can be contributed toward each allowable deduction, may change over time.

Figure 1. Disposition of personal net disposable income

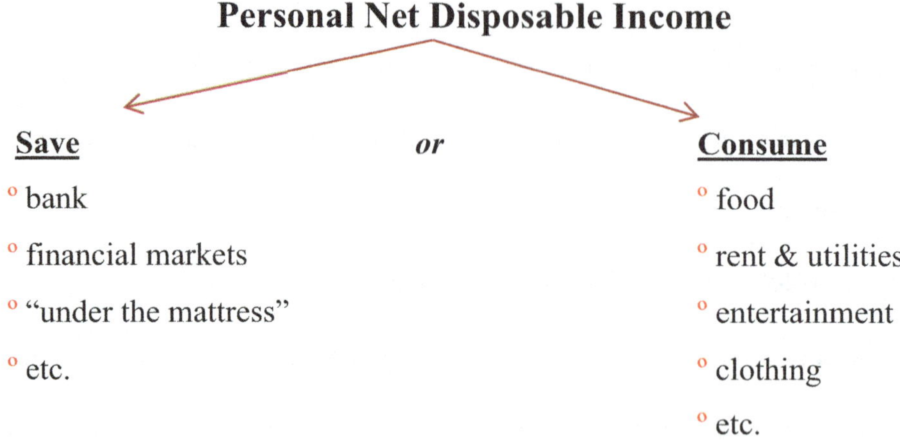

Generalizing this to the full population, any increase in gross income or decrease in deductions and/or taxes—keeping savings constant—will increase consumption. Per the expenditure approach formula [see equation (1.1)], an increase in consumption (C) will increase GDP. In contrast, any increases in deductions and taxes, keeping gross income and savings constant, will decrease consumption. Again, equation (1.1) demonstrates that a decrease in consumption will decrease GDP. Similarly, any increases in savings (holding gross income, deductions, and taxes constant) will decrease consumption and GDP.

Now that we understand the relationship between consumption, savings, consumer deductions, and consumer taxes in relation to GDP, we will explore calculating the magnitude of such changes.

MPC & MPS:

For an economy, we can measure the marginal (i.e., additional) impact of a $1 increase/decrease in consumption spending on disposable income. To do this calculation, we use the marginal propensity to consume (MPC) formula. The MPC can be calculated as the change in consumption spending divided by the change in disposable income: [34]

$$MPC = \Delta C / \Delta DI \qquad (1.2)$$

Where, Δ = change (value at period 1 – value at period 2)

C = consumption

And, DI = disposable income

We are assuming that the population can only spend or save disposable income; therefore, the limits of the MPC are between 0 and 1 (i.e., the MPC will fall between 0% and 100%).

Exercise 1: Calculating & Interpreting MPC

Assume you have 2015 and 2016 data for disposable income and consumption, as presented in the following table:

Year	**Disposable Income**	**Consumption**
2016	$200 trillion	$170 trillion
2015	$180 trillion	$160 trillion

Using this data, what is the marginal propensity to consume?

[34] MPC is also the slope of the consumer consumption curve (where disposable income is the X-variable and consumption spending is the Y-variable).

SOLUTION. *Utilizing equation (1.2), MPC = Δ C / Δ DI*

$$MPC = (170 - 160) / (200 - 180)$$

$$= 10 / 20$$

$$= 0.5, \text{ or, } 50\%$$

INTERPRETATION.

An MPC of 0.5 means that, on average, for every $1 trillion added to an economy's disposable income, consumers will spend an additional 50% of that $1 trillion (i.e., $500 billion). It also means that, on average, for every $1 trillion subtracted from an economy's disposable income (say, in the form of higher taxes), consumers will spend 50% less of that $1 trillion (i.e., disposable income will decrease by $500 billion).

Why is this important to know? As we will explore in subsequent chapters, the goal of the federal government is to grow and stabilize the economy. Therefore, knowing the MPC, if it needs to stimulate (or decelerate) the economy and it has a consumption spending target of "X" dollars, the government will know how much dollars it will need to inject into (or subtract from) the economy!

Similarly to exploring the magnitude of changes in consumer consumption, we can measure the magnitude to changes in consumer savings. For an economy, we can measure the marginal impact of a $1 increase/decrease in savings on GDP using the marginal propensity to save (MPS) formula. The MPS can be calculated as the change in savings divided by the change in disposable income:[35]

[35] MPS is also the slope of the savings curve (where disposable income is the X-variable and savings is the Y-variable).

$$MPS = \Delta S / \Delta DI \quad (1.3)$$

Where, Δ = change (value at period 1 – value at period 2)

S = savings

And, DI = disposable income

Remember, we are assuming that consumers can only spend or save disposable income. Therefore, the limits of the MPS—same as those of the MPC—are between 0 and 1 (i.e., the MPS will fall between 0% and 100%).

Exercise 2: Calculating & Interpreting MPS

Using the data from Exercise 1, we can create the same table and add the nation's savings (i.e., the difference between disposable income and consumption) for 2016 and 2015.

Year	**Disposable Income**	**Consumption**	**Savings** (Disposable Income – Consumption)
2016	$200 trillion	$170 trillion	$30 trillion
2015	$180 trillion	$160 trillion	$20 trillion

Having calculated the savings for 2016 and 2015 ($30 trillion and $20 trillion, respectively) and given the data in the table, what is the marginal propensity to save?

SOLUTION: *Utilizing equation (1.3), MPS = Δ S / Δ DI*

$$MPS = (30 - 20) / (200 - 180)$$

$$= 10 / 20$$

$$= 0.5, \text{ or, } 50\%$$

INTERPRETATION:

> *An MPS of 0.5 means that, on average, for every \$1 trillion added to disposable income, consumers will save an additional 50% of that \$1 trillion (i.e., \$500 billion). It also means that, on average, for every \$1 trillion subtracted from the economy's disposable income (say, in the form of higher taxes), consumer savings will decrease by 50% of that \$1 trillion (i.e., \$500 billion).*

With the assumption that consumers can only save or spend disposable income, we can state the following relationship: MPC + MPS = 1 (or 100%). Therefore, an alternative calculation of the MPS = 1 – MPC. (Similarly, an alternative calculation of the MPC = 1 – MPS).

As an example, if MPC = 0.7, then MPS = 0.3

$$\text{MPS} = 1 - \text{MPC}$$

$$= 1 - 0.7 = 0.3, \text{ or, } 30\%$$

In this case, for every \$1 increase in disposable income, consumers (on average) will save 30% on the additional \$1, or 30¢. They will also consume 70¢ on the additional \$1 of disposable income.

INVESTMENT SPENDING:

Investment spending is defined as "the total dollar value of investment spending by the business sector of the economy." Investment spending includes purchases made toward machinery, land, production inputs, infrastructure, consultancy, employee education/training, and more.

Please note that investment spending does NOT include investments made in the financial markets through the purchase of stocks, bonds, or derivative securities. This form of investment is called "capital formation" and is NOT considered an expense when calculating the expenditure approach to GDP; rather, it is considered a form of investment in capital. Remember, when we are calculating the expenditure approach to GDP, we are looking for all expenses (not incomes or capital) that emanate from each sector of the economy!

Per the expenditure approach formula [see equation (1.1)], when investment spending (I) increases, GDP will increase; and when investment spending decreases, GDP will decrease.

But what fuels investment spending? What factors cause businesses to increase or decrease their investment spending? A firm's investment spending is affected by interest rates, expected future level of real (adjusted for inflation) GDP, and the firm's current level of capacity in production.

FACTOR AFFECTING INVESTMENT SPENDING:

To explain the direction and impact of investment spending on GDP, we now turn to discuss, in detail, each of the three components.

1. **Interest rates:** An inverse relationship exists between interest rates and investment spending. If interest rates are low, then businesses can borrow funds at lower costs to expand their ventures—therefore, *ceteris paribus*, investment spending will increase. Alternatively, if interest rates are high, then firms face higher costs when borrowing funds to expand their business. Therefore, *ceteris paribus*, investment spending will decrease; overall, businesses will borrow less money. Interest rates will be discussed fully in later chapters.
2. **Expected future level of real GDP:** A direct relationship exists between expectations for the future level of real GDP and investment spending. On a national scale, when there are

expectations that the economy will bloom, investment spending increases. The same is true on a smaller scale: when businesses expect an increase in their future level of real income (such as ski resorts expecting lots of snow), their investment spending increases. In the case of ski resorts, investment spending may result in the hiring of more ski instructors or the purchase or lease of more skis—all in anticipation of the expected growth in their business. Alternatively, when there are expectations that the economy will weaken (possibly resulting in less sales, revenues, or profits), businesses will refrain from expanding, and thus investment spending will decrease.

3. **Current level of production capacity:** An inverse relationship exists between current level of production capacity and investment spending. *Ceteris paribus*, the lower the current level of production capacity, the higher the level of investment spending. In contrast, businesses will adjust their investment spending downward if they are already close to full capacity. Furthering the ski resort example, while the weather forecast predicts lots of snow in their area, businesses that already have a sufficient number of skis/instructors to handle the projected increase in guests, will not increase their investment spending. In contrast, businesses that are not at full capacity—have an sufficient number of skis/instructors to handle the increased capacity of prospective guests—will increase their investment spending.

Summarizing, investment spending (on average) will increase when interest rates are low, when the level of real GDP is expected to rise, and/or when the current level of production capacity is low. Per the calculation of GDP [see equation (1.1)], an increase in investment spending (I) will increase GDP. Conversely, investment spending (on average) will decrease when interest rates are high, when the level of real GDP is expected to decrease, and/or when the current level of production capacity is high. The same calculation demonstrates that a decrease in investment spending will decrease GDP.

FUNDING FOR "I" & EQUILIBRIUM:

So, where does the money to make these business expenditures come from? At the firm level, some possibilities of funding include a loan from the bank, money from a business savings account, angel investors, and venture capitalists. In addition, if the firm is publicly held, it can issue stocks and/or bonds.

At the national level, the money to fund business expenditures lies with consumer savings. Remember, financial institutions use consumers' deposits to make loans. So, unless consumers store their savings "under the mattress," so to speak, those savings fuel investment spending. When a closed economy (exclusive of the foreign sector) is in equilibrium, spending by the business sector (I) equals savings by the household sector (S). Worded differently, in a closed economy, equilibrium is found when I = S.[36]

GOVERNMENT SPENDING:

Government spending is defined as "the total dollar value of government spending on all goods and services."

A balanced budget for the government exists when taxation (T) is equal to government spending (G). For the fiscal year 2015, the federal budget of the United States was $3.8 trillion—or

[36] For the equilibrium condition in an open economy, see this chapter's section, "Equilibrium in an Open Economy".

approximately 21% of the US economy as measured by GDP. This translates to about $12,000 per person in the United States.[37]

For the government, taxes are an inflow of capital (i.e., receipts or money collected by the government), while government spending is an outflow of capital (i.e., outlays or money deducted from the government's budget to pay for goods or services). Throughout history, the United States has experienced periods of budget surpluses and deficits. Historical data of the US government's budget, in detail, can be found at the Government Publishing Office website.[38]

GOVERNMENT'S BUDGET:

We can summarize the government's budget as follows:

If $T > G$, this means Inflows > Outflows, which results in a Budget Surplus

$T < G$, this means Inflows < Outflows, which results in a Budget Deficit

In our calculation of GDP using equation (1.1), when government spending (G) increases, GDP increases; and when government spending decreases, GDP also decreases.

So, how does the federal government spend its money—the outflow of capital? Figure 4 shows the three main areas of fiscal spending: interest on debt, discretionary spending, and mandatory spending.

---

[37] Federal Spending: Where Does the Money Go, 2017.

[38] Budget of the United States Government, 2017.

Figure 4. 2015 United States federal government's total budget (in billion dollars)

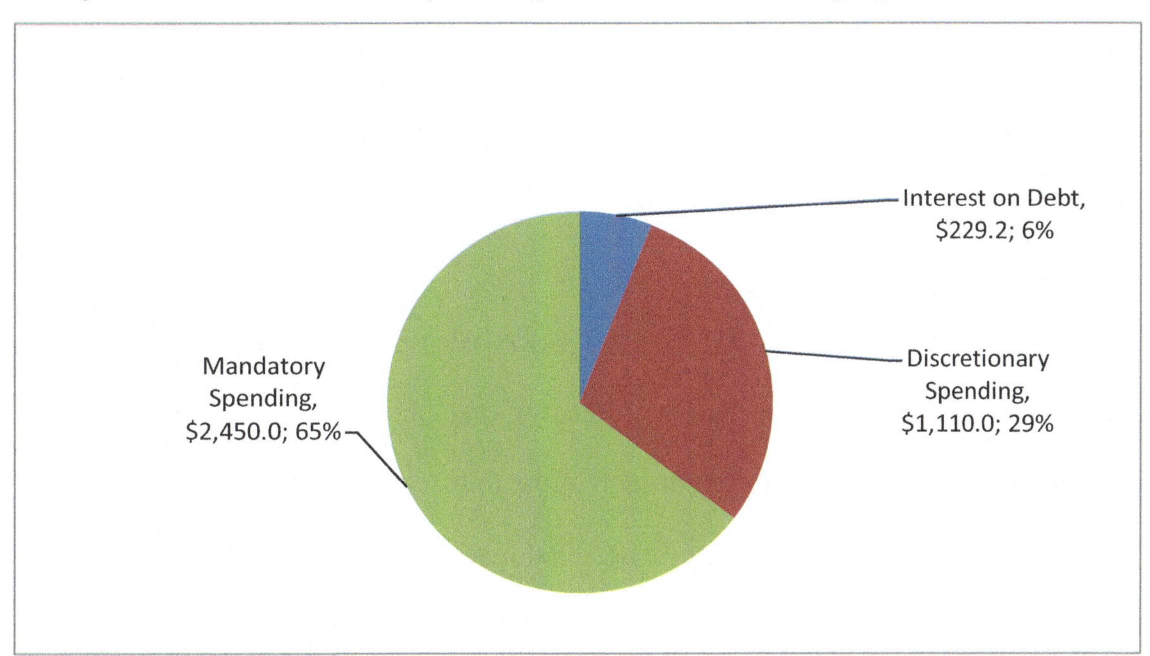

Source: Federal Spending: Where Does the Money Go, 2017.

The federal government's mandatory spending, the largest expenditure of the government's budget (65%) is comprised of spending in the following categories: Social Security, unemployment & labor; Medicare & health; food & agriculture; veterans' benefits; transportation; plus, a miscellaneous category.

The federal government's discretionary spending (29%) is comprised of the following categories: military (its largest percentage of discretionary expenditure); government; education; [additional] Medicare & health; [additional] veterans' benefits; housing & community; international affairs; energy & environment; science; [additional] transportation; and [additional] food & agriculture.

In 2015, the remaining 2.6% of the federal government's total budget was devoted to paying the interest on its debt.

So, while increases in government spending (the "outflow" of capital for the government) increase GDP, how do increases in taxation (the "inflow" of capital for the government) affect GDP? Where does taxation "fit into" the calculation of GDP?

TAXATION'S EFFECT ON ALL 4 SECTORS OF THE ECONOMY:

While a change in taxation does not directly affect the calculation of the expenditure approach to GDP, taxation does play an integral part in each of the four sectors of the economy:

1. **Household sector**: An increase in personal taxes will decrease net disposable income, consumption, and—*ceteris paribus*—GDP. And a decrease in personal taxes will increase net disposable income, consumption, and—*ceteris paribus*—GDP.
2. **Business sector**: An increase in business taxes will increase business expenses, and if companies cannot pass along the increase to its customers (i.e., via a price increase), business spending will decrease. In sum, *ceteris paribus*, an increase in business taxes will cause a decrease in GDP. Alternatively, a decrease in business taxes will increase business spending and, *ceteris paribus*, increase GDP.
3. **Government sector**: While there is no a priori reason for the government to balance its budget, political and economic pressures may push the government to increase or decrease taxes (i.e., in the form of tax abatements, which are generally geared to firms in the form of property taxes in order to encourage economic development; or tax refunds). A full discussion of fiscal policy will be presented in Chapter 11.
4. **Foreign sector**: Should the government increase taxes on imported products (i.e., a tariff), imports will decrease, and vice versa. See the next section ("Net Exports") for a more detailed explanation.

In sum, while an increase in taxes will result in a government budget surplus, an increase in taxes in the household and business sectors, *ceteris paribus*, will likely decrease GDP. In contrast, an increase in taxes in the foreign sector of the economy will, *ceteris paribus*, increase GDP.

NET EXPORTS:

"Net exports" is defined as "the net dollar value of total export expenditures by the economy as a whole." It can be calculated as follows: total exports (Ex) – total imports (Im).

"Exports" refer to the total dollar value of products or services produced within our nation's borders that will be sent abroad for consumption abroad. When we export products or services, the dollar value of these products comes into our country and net exports increase. So, if a US company sells its products to Japan; it receives payments in exchange for the products. The receipts of these payments will result, *ceteris paribus,* in an increase in total exports, net exports and GDP.

In contrast, "imports" refer to the total dollar value of goods or services purchased from abroad and brought into the United States for consumption in the United States. When we import products or services from abroad, money flows out of our country. As a result, *ceteris paribus,* net exports and GDP decreases.

We can summarize the effect of imports and exports on net exports (NE) and GDP as follows:

if $Ex > Im$, then NE rises, and GDP rises;

and if $Ex < Im$, then NE declines and GDP declines.

But what affects net exports? Net exports are primarily affected by what we refer to as "barriers to trade," which include government regulations, government taxes, and exchange rates. The following is a discussion of government trade regulations and taxes, but we will turn to a full explanation of exchange rates in Chapter 8.

TRADE REGULATIONS:

In the market of net exports, government rules and regulations take the form of restrictions, tariffs, and quotas.

- A **restriction** is a government rule/regulation that prevents or restricts the quantity of a product or service that is imported (e.g., imports of steel from China) or exported (e.g., trade to embargoed nations). The US Department of Homeland Security's Customs and Border Protection agency lists specific trade requirements that must be met.[39] It also offers a full listing of prohibited (i.e., forbidden by US law, such as absinthe—a mind-altering substance) and restricted (i.e., in need of licenses/permits, such as the importation of animal by-products) items.[40]
- A **tariff** is a government tax that is imposed on an imported product or service. Therefore, a tariff affects the price (usually by an increase) of an imported good or service; it is considered a restriction on price.
- A **quota** is a government regulation that restricts trade by placing a maximum amount on the quantity of a product or service being imported. Therefore, a quota affects the quantity (usually by a decrease) of an imported good or service; it is considered a restriction on quantity.

[39] The Department of Homeland Security, 2017.

[40] Prohibited and Restricted Items, 2018.

To conclude, calculating the expenditure approach to GDP (GDP = C + I + G + NE),

GDP will increase directly with an increase in C, I, G, or NE—or when S↓, T↓, Ex↑, or Im↓; and,

GDP will decrease directly with a decrease in C, I, G, or NE—or when S↑, T↑, Ex↓, or Im↑.

But what equilibrium conditions are true in an open economy?

EQUILIBRIUM IN AN OPEN ECONOMY:

A country is said to have an "open economy" when there are economic activities *(i.e., actions that may involve the production/manufacturing, distribution, and/or consumption of goods/services)* that occur between that country's economic agents *(i.e., where these agents can take the form of either individuals or companies)* and economic agents outside that country. This assumes that funds, investments, merchandise, managerial exchanges, and services can flow across the border. In other words, an open economy means that international trade can occur—that a country can import and export products/services. According to the World Bank Report, the countries with the highest exports of goods and services (expressed as a percentage of GDP) in 2017 included the United Arab Emirates, Vietnam, Ireland, Singapore, the Hong Kong SAR, China, and Luxembourg—at 100.4%, 101.5%, 120%, 173.3%, 188%, and 230%, respectively.[41] Out of 189 World Bank member countries (plus 28 other economies with populations greater than 30,000), these six countries, with exports greater than 100% of GDP, would be considered the most "open" economies of 2017.

This contrasts with a closed economy whereby international trade and finance do not (or cannot) take place. According to the World Bank Report, the countries with the lowest reported exports of

[41] Exports of Good & Services, 2018.

goods and services (expressed as a percentage of GDP) in 2017 included Ethiopia, Pakistan, Sudan, Nepal, and Kiribati—at 7.7%, 8.2%, 9.7%, 9.8%, and 9.9%, respectively. These five countries, with exports less than 10% of GDP, would be considered the most "closed" economies of 2017.

So, what is the equilibrium condition in an open economy (with the incorporation of the foreign sector)?

LEAKAGES & INJECTIONS:

For an open economy in equilibrium, we can state that "injections should equal leakages." "Injections" are any increases in consumer spending that increase a country's aggregate output and national income. Injections are viewed as the inflows of capital into an economy, which are represented in the GDP calculation as "investments (I) + government spending (G) + exports (Ex)." In contrast, "leakages" are any increases in consumer spending that decrease domestic aggregate output and national income. Leakages are viewed as the outflows of capital from an economy, which are represented in the GDP calculation as "savings (S) + taxes (T) + imports (Im)."

Thus, in an open economy in equilibrium, injections are equal to leakages.

Mathematically, we can write: (I + G + Ex) = (S + T + Im).[42]

[42] As mentioned previously, this equilibrium condition contrasts with the equilibrium condition for a closed economy, where spending by the business sector (I) equals savings by the household sector (S).

Balance of Trade:

The balance of trade, for any given period, can be defined as "the difference in value between a country's imports and exports (i.e., Ex – Im)" and is used to measure the relative strength of a country's economy.

We can rearrange the previous formula for an open economy in equilibrium by expressing the balance of trade (i.e., net exports) as a function of net domestic savings:

$$Ex - Im = (S - I) + (T - G)$$

Where, (S–I) represents the private sector saving

And, (T – G) represents the public sector saving (i.e., the government's budget surplus)

Therefore, for an open economy in equilibrium, we find that the balance of trade should be equal to the savings of both the private and public sectors.

Economic Growth Measured by GDP over Time:

We can use the expenditure approach to GDP to calculate an economy's income at a point in time and its income growth over a period. Using the GDP formula (GDP = C + I + G + NE), we can conclude, as stated previously, that GDP will rise if consumption, investment spending, government spending, and exports increase; or if savings or imports decrease. Alternatively, GDP will decrease if consumption, investment spending, government spending, and exports decrease; or if savings or imports increase.

Overall, the GDP of an economy follows what we call "the business cycle"—the periods of fluctuations (i.e., "ups and downs") over time.

THE BUSINESS CYCLE:

In analyzing the business cycle, we note that it has four segments: recovery, prosperity or peak, recession, and trough or depression.

The "recovery phase" of the business cycle occurs when the economy is doing well (i.e., expanding) and GDP is on the rise. When the economy hits the peak of the business cycle, we call this phase "prosperity" or the "peak." Then, as with anything that rises and reaches a peak, when the economy starts to "slide down" (i.e., contracting) and GDP is on the decline, we call this the "recession" phase of the business cycle. Lastly, when the economy reaches its lowest point of the business cycle, we call this phase the "trough" or "depression."

These four phases repeat over time. Figure 5 shows GDP graphed over time and highlights the phases of the business cycle. If we drew a line halfway between these fluctuations, the slope of the line over time (or trendline) would measure the average growth (or decline) in GDP. We would hope that, over time, this trendline would slope upwards, i.e., GDP would be growing!

Figure 5. The business cycle over time

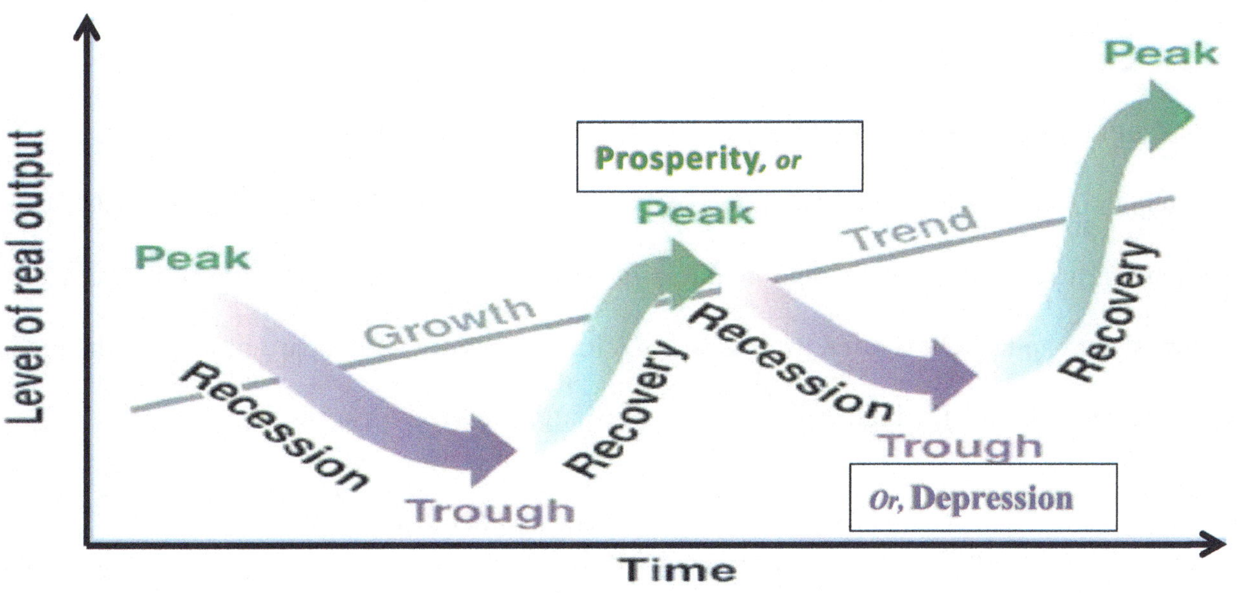

Now you might ask, do these fluctuations have to be large (i.e., have a large standard deviation from the GDP's mean value) or can they be small (i.e., have a small standard deviation from the GDP's mean value)? Should the fluctuation of these four phases remain constant over time? The answer to these questions is no. The magnitude of the four phases of the business cycle will fluctuate over time. Throughout history, we have seen very high spikes (prolonged periods of prosperity) as well as deep downward spikes (prolonged periods of recession/depression). A nation prefers to experience very small fluctuations (a low standard deviation) among the four phases of the business cycle as well as an upward sloping GDP trend line over time. In Chapter 9, we will discuss the downfall of being at the prosperity phase, the downfall of being at the trough phase, and how we can tell which phase of the business cycle we are in.

However, when we want to compare the growth or decline in GDP between countries, we must acknowledge that, *ceteris paribus*, a larger country will have a higher GDP than a smaller country with fewer people. So, to compare "relative" GDP growth or decline, given unequal populations, we look at the per capita GDP of each country.

PER CAPITA GDP & ITS TREND FOR THE US, EU & EMU COUNTRIES:

"Per capita GDP", literally translated to "per head" GDP, is the GDP of the nation divided by its population. It represents the average total output for a country for each member of its workforce. At times, per capita GDP is referenced as a proxy for the country's "standard of living"; the higher the per capita income, the higher the standard of living, and vice versa.

Figure 6 shows the per capita GDP, expressed in US Dollars, from 1960 to 2014 for the United States, the Economic and Monetary Union (EMU)[43], countries (i.e., those that have adopted the euro) and the non-EMU countries (i.e., those that have not adopted the euro) of the European Union (EU).[44]

---

[43] As of 2014, the EMU countries are (in alphabetical order): Austria, Belgium, Cyprus, Estonia, Finland, France, Germany, Greece, Ireland, Italy, Latvia, Luxembourg, Malta, the Netherlands, Portugal, Slovakia, Slovenia, and Spain. These countries have adopted the euro.

[44] As of 2014, the EU/non-EMU countries are (in alphabetical order): Bulgaria, Croatia, the Czech Republic, Denmark, Hungary, Lithuania, Poland, Romania, Sweden, and the United Kingdom. These countries have not yet adopted the euro.

Figure 6. Average per capita GDP (in US dollars)

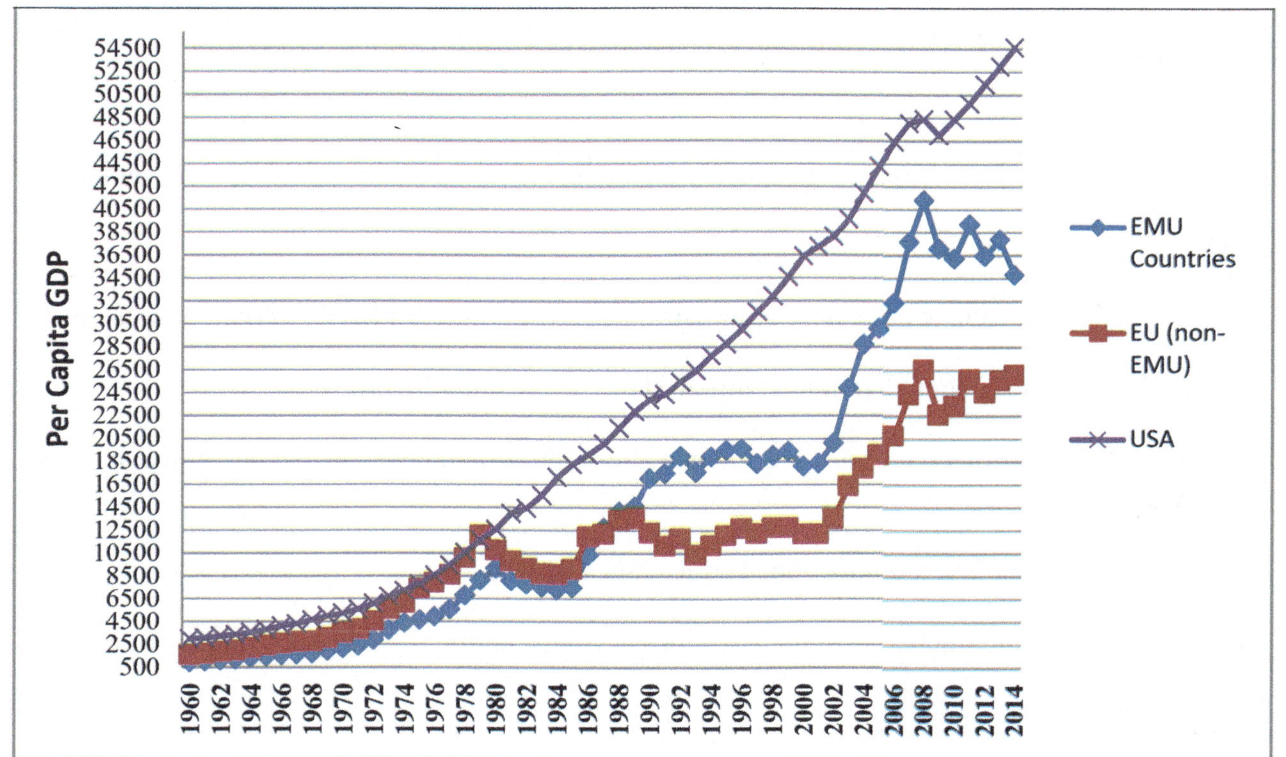

Source: World Development Indicators

After the first phase of EMU in 1990, the average per capita GDP of the EMU countries is higher than the average per capita GDP of the EU countries. Therefore, while monetary unification had a mixed effect on the individual countries that adopted the euro, overall, we can see a positive impact on their average per capita GDP. (For a detailed study of monetary unification, see Lo Re, Mary & Cathyann Tully 2011.)

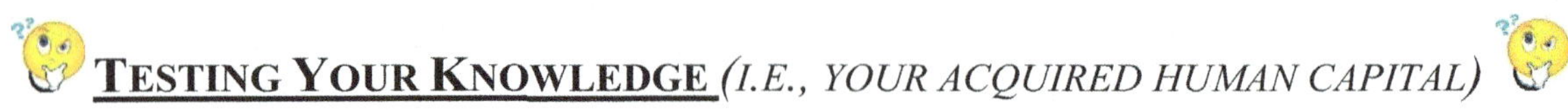

TESTING YOUR KNOWLEDGE *(I.E., YOUR ACQUIRED HUMAN CAPITAL)*

Determine whether the following questions/statements are true or false. If false, can you explain why?

1. John, a US citizen, works only in Australia. Is the value added to production from his employment, only included in the United States' GNP calculations?
2. The calculation of GDP does not include the unpaid maintenance of your house by your spouse.
3. In an open economy, are injections and leakages related as $(I + G + Ex) = (S + T + Im)$?
4. Regardless of the fluctuations in the business cycle, a nation's goal is to see an upward trend in their aggregate income over time.
5. If your country is ranked among the "spender" countries, it implies that your country's marginal propensity to consume is higher than that of a "saver" country.

CHAPTER 8. FOREIGN EXCHANGE RATES[45]

An exchange rate is defined as "the value of one currency in relation to another currency." The US dollar is the United States' currency, and the currency's value is measured by its exchange rate. The value of a currency is determined by the demand and supply of the currency. When the value of the currency increases, we say the currency "appreciates" or there is an "appreciation" of the currency (i.e., the US dollar is "strong").[46] When the value of the currency decreases, we say the currency "depreciates" or there is a "depreciation" of the currency (i.e., the US dollar is "weak").[47]

ECONOMIC IMPLICATIONS OF A STRONG/WEAK CURRENCY:

Is a strong currency good for a country? (Note that a strong currency results when there exists a stronger demand for that currency.) Or would a country fare better if it had a weak currency?

The strength or weakness of a country's currency has economic implications for net exports, the financial market, and interest rates.

If a currency is weak relative to another currency, exports increase, and imports decrease; this increases net exports. An increase in net exports, *ceteris paribus*, will lead to an increase in GDP,

---

[45] I would like to thank Dr. Richard N. LaRocca for his editorial contributions to this entire chapter.

[46] Please note that the term "appreciation" is used under a floating exchange rate system. However, under a fixed exchange rate system, where the value of a country's currency increases in relation to another currency, this is called a **revaluation** of currency.

[47] Please note that the term "depreciation" is used under a floating exchange rate system. However, under a fixed exchange rate system, where the value of a country's currency decreases in relation to another currency, this is called a **devaluation** of currency.

thus having an "expansionary" effect on the economy. This is one reason why the Chinese yuan was devalued against the US dollar for many years.[48] When China devalues its currency against the US dollar, it can export more products to the United States without having to decrease the product prices.

A further example can be seen in a 2017 study conducted by LaRocca et al. The research examined whether six EMU countries used the euro as a currency manipulation to strengthen their economies via cheaper exports. The study showed that if the EMU countries had retained their respective currencies, a forecasted currency revaluation was found for France, Italy, and Germany; while a forecasted devaluation was found for Greece, Portugal, and Spain.

If a currency is strong relative to another currency, exports decrease and imports increase; this decreases net exports. A decrease in net exports, *ceteris paribus*, will lead to a decrease in GDP, thus having a "contractionary" effect on the economy. Furthering the Chinese currency example, when (in 2017) the value of the Chinese yuan increased in relation to the US dollar, The Wall Street Journal headline read "yuan's surprise strength handcuffs China's ability to manage its economic decline"![49]

In the financial market, the dollar historically moves in the opposite direction of the stock market. So, we often see that when the US dollar is strong, the Dow Jones Industrial Average (i.e., the "Dow") is down; and when the US dollar is weak, the Dow is up! This negative correlation is primarily due to the fact that when the US dollar is weak, it boosts the earnings of multinational

[48] Rosenfeld, 2016.

[49] Wei & Vaishampayan, 2017.

corporations, strengthening their stock values overseas. Naturally, the opposite effect is generally seen with a strong US dollar. However, while historically, this inverse relationship between the US $ and the Dow has been shown, in the article "Market Mythbusting: The "Strong" Correlation between USD and US Stocks" Ani Salama (2015) shows that a positive correlation now exists between the US $ and the Dow! So, in the next decades, will a direct or indirect relationship exist between the financial market and the US $? It will be interesting to see which relationship will dominate!

Effects on Interest Rates:

Generally, when the US dollar starts to appreciate in value, the interest rate rises. But rising interest rates attract an inflow of foreign capital. This arises as there will generally be an increased demand for the US dollar to capture the higher rate of interest. However, if the country is expanding too quickly (i.e., in terms of GDP or economic growth), and the government sees an overall increase in prices,[50] an inflow of foreign capital will have an opposing effect on the economy. This is because at the prosperity phase of the business cycle, the government's goal would be to slowdown/contract the economy (in order to avoid inflationary pressures)![51]

In contrast, when the US dollar starts to depreciate in value, the interest rate falls in an effort to stimulate exports. But falling interest rates cause an outflow of foreign capital. An outflow of foreign capital will have an opposing effect on the economy that is trying to expand! (A more detailed explanation of these "counter" effects can be found in Chapter 11.)

---

[50] This occurs when the economy is leading toward the peak or prosperity phase of the business cycle-as graphically seen in Chapter 7, fig. 5)

[51] An explanation of inflation and its measurements is found in Chapter 9.

So, how do you "read" an interest rate, and how do you interpret it?

Reading the Exchange Rate & Meaning:

Take the following quiz to see if you truly know the meaning of the exchange rate between two currencies—the US dollar and the euro.

Quiz: Reading the Exchange Rate:

If the euro/US dollar exchange rate equals 0.94, what does this mean?

a. 1 euro is equivalent to (exchanged for) 0.94 US dollars.

b. 1 US dollar is equivalent to 0.94 euros.

The answer to this quiz is *b.*

Therefore, when trying to find the US dollar equivalent of any currency (i.e., in this case, the euro), remember that the US dollar is the denominator of the equation!

As another example, an exchange rate of 1.48 means you will receive 1.48 euros for every 1 US dollar.

The Foreign Exchange Market:

Exchange rates change every day because currencies are traded on the foreign exchange market (i.e., called the "forex" for short) where the price of a currency is determined by demand and supply for that currency.[52] The forex market is the market in which participants can buy, sell, exchange, and speculate [on] currencies. It enables currency conversion for international trade and

[52] Example of changing exchange rates on same date, different years: On June 27, 2017, the Euro/US$ exchange rate = 0.8817; same date in 2016, it = 0.9076; and same date in 2015, it = 0.8956.

investments. The market makers include banks, commercial companies, central/national banks, investment management firms, hedge funds, and retail forex brokers and investors. The foreign exchange market—open 24 hours a day, 5 days a week—is considered the largest financial market in the world, and its characteristics include high liquidity and leverage (i.e., a loan given to an investor by a broker to enhance profits/gains).

What determines exchange rates (or, say, the value of the US dollar)?

FACTORS AFFECTING EXCHANGE RATES:

Exchange rates are derived by demand and supply forces determined by five primary factors: relative price differences & purchasing power parity, interest rates & monetary supply, productivity & balance of payments, investor psychology, and exchange rate policy.

- **Relative price differences & purchasing power parity**

The theory of purchasing power parity (PPP) suggests that with no barriers to trade, the price for identical products are expected to be the same across countries; otherwise, traders would buy low and sell high! This theory suggests that in the long run, exchange rates should move (either up or down) in each country so as to equalize the price of identical baskets/grouping of goods/services. In general, while the theory does not apply to an individual product or service, the Big Mac Index created in 1986, can be seen as an indicator of the "misalignment" in the theory of PPP. This index is often used to gauge whether a currency is over or undervalued. For instance, the following misalignment of PPP was reported in July 2018 by The Economist stating: "A Big Mac costs £3.19 in Britain and US$5.51 in the United States. Therefore, the implied exchange rate is 0.58 [i.e., 3.19 / 5.51 = 0.58]. The difference between this [rate] and the actual exchange rate, 0.75, suggests the British pound is 23.2% undervalued."[53] Mathematically, for PPP to hold, an actual exchange rate of 0.75 would mean that the Big Mac in Britain should cost £4.13 (i.e., 0.75 × $5.51) instead of £3.19. So, the misalignment in PPP can be calculated as follows: [(£3.19 – £4.13) / £4.13] = -0.232, and expressed as a percent = -23.2%. As the resultant is negative, the British pound is said to be undervalued.

- **Interest rates & monetary supply**

If a country has high interest rates relative to other countries, it will attract foreign fund investments. A high interest rate will also increase demand for the country's currency; therefore, putting pressure to increase the currency's exchange rate value.

The article "*Interest Rates & the FX Market*" does a great job in explaining the relationship between interest rates, currency values, and the supply of money. As Jeremy Wagner (2012) states in this Daily Forex article, "High and increasing rates at the beginning of an economic expansion can generate growth and value in a currency. On the other hand, low and lowering rates may represent a country experiencing difficult economic conditions which is reflective in a reduction of the currency value."

- **Productivity & balance of payments**

The balance of payments is a country's international transaction statement that captures the current account plus the capital account entries. The current account is the net payments from trade in

---

[53] Big Mac Index, 2018.

goods, trade in services, and net income flows; and, the capital account is the capital and financial account net balances from consumers, businesses and the government.

A favorable balance of payments, resulting from a nation's increased demand for products/services, generally leads to an increase in the value of the nation's currency.[54] Likewise, an unfavorable balance of payments, resulting from a nation's decreased demand for products/services, generally leads to a decrease in the value of the nation's currency. In sum, a change in the balance of payments can cause fluctuations in the exchange rate between a country's currency and foreign currencies.[55]

- **Investor psychology**

Two examples demonstrate how exchange rates are affected by investor movements in the foreign exchange market: the bandwagon effect and the capital flight effect.

When investors all move in a particular direction, it is called the "investment bandwagon effect" or the information cascade effect. In the financial market, as suggested by Keiichi Shima (2016, 30), the bandwagon effect can be seen in firms with smaller market shares: "That is, smaller firms rely on rival investments as a signal of market opportunities." Thus, smaller firms tend to follow the same investment patterns as their rival firms—possibly from the fear of missing out.

---

[54] In my 2011 study, *"Impact of the Global Financial Crisis on the EU and Euro Area vs. the USA"* published in the China-USA Business Review, I showed that the current account balances (expressed as a percentage of GDP for the period 2000 to 2014), for both the US and the EU countries, experienced a deficit. In contrast, China reported positive current account balances over the entire period peaking at 11% in 2007. This supports the Chinese government's intervention in the foreign exchange market to devalue its currency against the US Dollar.

[55] However, please note that the balance of payments may not impact the exchange rate in a fixed-rate system if central banks adjust currency flows to offset the international exchange of funds.

When many investors exchange domestic currency for foreign currency, it is called the capital flight effect. "Capital flight, in economics, occurs when assets or money rapidly flow out of a country due to an event of economic consequence." (Capital Flight, 2018). An example would be an increase in the government debt default rate causing investors to lower their valuation and lose confidence in the country's economic strength. This may be accompanied by a drop in the exchange rate, making it expensive for the defaulting country to import goods or services from abroad. A prime example of an international capital flight crisis occurred in December 1994 when the Mexican government suddenly devalued the peso against the US dollar. A recount of the Mexican peso crisis can be found in Lustig's June 1995 Brookings Report.

- **Exchange rate policy**

Exchange rate policies set by a country's government can be floating or flexible (i.e., determined by supply and demand conditions), clean or free (i.e., determined by a pure market solution), dirty or managed (i.e., determined by government intervention), fixed or target (i.e., determined relative to other currencies), crawling band (i.e., having specified upper/lower bounds of fluctuation), or pegged (i.e., linked to a key currency of another country).

PEGGED *VS.* FLOATING CURRENCY POLICIES:

A country's government can choose to intervene in the setting of its exchange rates by "pegging" its currency against another currency. Alternatively, it can choose not to intervene by "floating" its currency against another currency. Floating exchange rates vary according to market forces.

In contrast, a pegged (or "fixed") exchange rate is fixed (i.e., set) between two currencies—the pegging country's government artificially fixes the exchange rate so that there is no daily value fluctuation relative to the other currency.

So, why would a country peg one currency to another? Pegging allows stability in the exchange rate between the pegging country's currency and a major currency. This pegging policy can be enforced through currency controls or influenced through the Federal Reserve's open market operations[56] in the foreign exchange market. However, the pegging government's central bank must be active in maintaining the fixed exchange rate to mitigate changes in supply and demand for its currency; and the central bank must hold large foreign currency reserves in order to defend and uphold the peg.

A developing nation with a small, unstable economy may utilize a pegged currency in order to control inflation, keep export prices stable, and allow its central bank to benefit from the credibility of its pegged counterpart. But, once again, this can only occur if there are sufficient capital resources to maintain the peg.

EXAMPLES OF PEGGED CURRENCIES:[57]

As of February 2015, there are 17 countries that have pegged their currency to the euro:

Benin (XOF), Bosnia (BAM), Bulgaria (BGN), Burkina Faso (XOF), Cameroon (XAF), the Central African Republic (XAF), Chad (XAF), Denmark (DKK), Equatorial Guinea (XAF),

[56] See Chapter 11, the 3rd "tool" of monetary policy for a full description of open market operations.

[57] I would like to thank my colleague Prof. Ian Wise for providing me with the lists of currencies pegged against the euro and the US dollar.

Gabon (XAF), Guinea-Bissau (XOF), Ivory Coast (XOF), Mali (XOF), Niger (XOF), the Congo (XAF), Senegal (XOF), and Togo (XOF).[58]

Furthermore, there are 12 countries that have pegged their currency to the US dollar: Bahrain (BHD), Cuba (CUC), Djibouti (DJF), Eritrea (ERN), Hong Kong (HKD), Jordan (JOD), Lebanon (LBP), Oman (OMR), Panama (PAB), Qatar (QAR), the United Arab Emirates (AED), and Venezuela (VEB). However, please note that this may no longer be the case for Venezuela given their 2017 inflation crisis.[59]

ANCHOR CURRENCY & COUNTRY EXAMPLES:

In addition to pegged/floating currency policies, some countries faced with many economic difficulties (e.g., extremely high levels of inflation, increased poverty, and decreased currency values) have adopted stronger "anchor" currencies as their own. This is called "dollarization" and allows countries to gain stability over the use of their own currencies.

As an example, countries that use the US dollar as their medium of exchange include the British Virgin Islands, Ecuador, El Salvador, Guam, the Northern Mariana Islands, the Marshall Islands, Micronesia, Palau, Puerto Rico, Timor-Leste, Turks and Caicos, the Virgin Islands, and Zimbabwe.[60] Other examples of countries adopting anchor currencies include Liechtenstein (the Swiss franc), the West Bank and Gaza (the Israeli shekel), Belgium (the now-defunct French franc), and Luxembourg (the now-defunct Belgian franc).

---

[58] "XAF" represents the Central African CFA franc; "XOF" represents the West African CFA franc.

[59] You may want to read Patrick Gillespie's November 2017 article "'Death spiral': 4,000% inflation in Venezuela."

[60] For a greater understanding of the pros and cons of dollarization, see Alesina & Barro, 2001.

A brief history of exchange rates and monetary systems can be seen in figure 2.

Figure 2. A brief history of exchange rates & monetary systems

1870–1914	Gold standard system: value of currency fixed to price of gold
1946–1971	Bretton Woods system: all currencies pegged at a fixed rate to US$
1971	United States abandons pegging to gold: $1 = 1/35^{th}$ ounce of gold; US$ floats
1973	Smithsonian Agreement: most major currencies float (**$ £ ¥**)
	Post–Bretton Woods system: flexible exchange rate regimes
2000	Introduction of euro (€) and end of DM, FF, lira, peseta, etc.

CONTROLLING FOR RISK—NONFINANCIAL & FINANCIAL:

Any individual, company, or government that engages in a transaction involving another currency runs the risk of currency exchange—the potential for loss associated with the fluctuations of the foreign exchange market.

So how do nonfinancial companies deal with currency risk without engaging in the financial or forex market? Two strategies are offered:

1. **Invoice a product in own currency**—thus avoiding exchange rates altogether.
2. **Engage in strategic hedging**—doing business in different currency zones abroad to offset any currency losses in one region with currency gains in another region.

How do companies deal with currency risk while engaging in the financial or forex market? There are many strategies used to reduce exchange rate risk using the financial markets. A company can engage in **currency hedging** (e.g., swap currency, forward contracts, buy foreign currency options, buy gold, buy spot contracts, etc.). One example of currency hedging is the carry-trade strategy.

CARRY-TRADE STRATEGY:

See figure 3 for a full description of how global traders use this strategy to hedge the risk associated with exchange rates losses.

Figure 3. Value of currency & interest rates carry-trade strategy[61]

Using the carry trade strategy, an investor borrows a given amount in a low-interest rate currency (the "funding" currency, i.e., the US dollar). S/he converts the funds into a high-interest rate currency (the "target" currency, i.e., the euro) and lends the resulting amount in the target currency (the Euro) at the higher interest rate. In other words, this strategy usually involves borrowing one currency at a very low rate and investing it in another country where interest rates are higher. The difference between the two rates is the profit! The risk is that the investor is essentially betting that the currency s/he borrowed will remain weak. If it gains strength, s/he risks erasing some or all her/his profits on the deal.

Empirical evidence shows that currencies that are at a forward premium (i.e., where the future spot exchange rate is greater than the current) and that, correspondingly, have low interest rates, tend (on average) to depreciate, as the theory of interest rate parity conditions predicts. (The opposite condition is also true.) This anomaly, then, implies that an investor who engages in a carry trade strategy is quite likely to make predictable profits from two sources: 1) the interest rate differential between the two currencies and 2) the appreciation of the high-interest rate currency originally bought at a forward discount.

As an example, the Japanese yen (which has low interest rates) has been used to buy currencies such as the US dollar and the Australian dollar (which at times have high interest rates). When the JPY is used for the carry trade strategy, the United States/Australia is the beneficiary of the investment dollars. When the US/Australian dollar is used instead, those investments are going elsewhere—which is detrimental for the growth of the US/Australian economy.

[61] For full details, see Frankel, 2017.

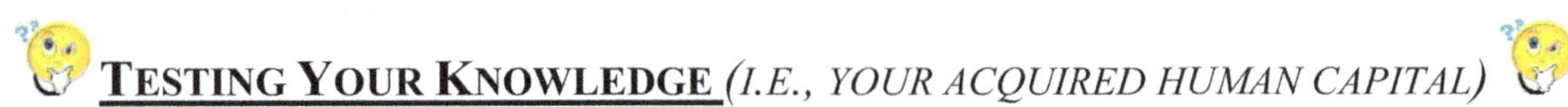

TESTING YOUR KNOWLEDGE *(I.E., YOUR ACQUIRED HUMAN CAPITAL)*

Determine whether the following statements/questions are true or false. If false, can you explain why?

1. A “revaluation of currency” occurs when, under a floating exchange rate system, the value of a country’s currency increases in relation to another currency.
2. A positive consequence of a strong currency is an increase in GDP.
3. If the US dollar/British pound = 0.89, does this mean that $1 is equivalent to £0.89?
4. For the countries pegging their currency to a country’s “major” currency, does “pegging” cause instability in the exchange rate for these “pegging” countries?
5. There are no effective strategies to offset the risks associated with currency exchanges.

CHAPTER 9. *UNEMPLOYMENT* VS. *INFLATION, DEFLATION & ECONOMIC INDICATORS*

In Chapter 7, we reviewed the four phases of the business cycle—recovery, prosperity/peak, recession, and depression/trough—and asked a question: what are the pitfalls when an economy is at the trough or at the peak (the polar opposites) of the business cycle? The quick answer is unemployment and inflation, respectively. In this chapter, we will turn our attention to understanding these two economic conditions, the distinction between deflation & disinflation, and economic indicators (i.e., what variables are used to help us determine where we are on the business cycle).

UNDERSTANDING UNEMPLOYMENT:

Unemployment may be generally defined as "the unintentional state of not being employed, or without work"! So, does this mean that a stay-at-home dad or mom is considered unemployed? What about a billionaire who has decided not to work? Is s/he considered unemployed?[62] What about a graduate student who has decided to leave his/her job to pursue an accelerated MBA degree program? Is this person considered unemployed? In order to answer these questions, we must understand how the government defines and categorizes unemployment.

In simple terms, what follows is the process used to calculate the unemployment figures. First, we can divide the total population into two groups—people who are in the labor force (i.e., eligible or considered eligible to work) and people who are not in the labor force.

[62] Take, for example, the winner of the $1.6 billion Mega Millions jackpot on Tuesday, October 23, 2018. If that person decided to quit his/her job, is this person considered "unemployed"?

Individuals who are "not in the labor force" can be categorized as follows:

- **Less than 16 years of age**

  In the United States, children are required to attend school (or be homeschooled) up to the age of 16 years; therefore, as full-time students, they cannot be employed on a full-time basis and cannot be considered as full participants in the labor force.

- **Institutionalized**

  If an individual, regardless of age, is in an institution, s/he cannot be employed or look for a job; therefore, institutionalized individuals cannot be considered as participants in the labor force. Examples include people that are incarcerated or in long-term health facilities.

- **Disabled**

  Disabled individuals that do not fall under the guidelines set by the Americans with Disabilities Act (ADA) are not eligible for full-time employment; therefore, they cannot be considered as participants in the labor force.[63]

- **In the Armed Forces**

  If an individual is in any branch of the Armed Forces, s/he is considered employed; therefore, members of the Armed Forces cannot be considered as participants in the public labor force.

- **In school**

  If an individual is a full-time student, s/he is not considered as a participant in the labor force—as their "job" is to be in school studying!

---

[63] The ADA protects disabled individuals in receiving equal rights of employment. Companies with 15 or more employees must reasonably accommodate the disabilities of qualified applicants/employees unless undue hardships would result.

- **Retired**

  By definition, a retiree is someone who has removed him/herself from the labor force.

- **"Discouraged"**

  A "discouraged worker" is someone who actively looked for a job, could not find one (either because of a poor economy or a lack of skills required in the economy), and became so discouraged about the prospects of employment that s/he stopped looking for a job. Discouraged workers no longer seek employment; therefore, they cannot be considered as participants in the labor force.

If you are "not in the labor force" (i.e., you do not meet the criteria under any of the previously listed categories), then you are considered "in the labor force." But does that necessarily mean you have a job? No, that is only one subcategory of an individual who is "in the labor force." So, if you are in the labor force, then you can either be employed (working for a company/individual or self-employed) or not employed.

UNEMPLOYMENT CATEGORIES:

If you are not employed, the government classifies reasons for unemployment under four categories: seasonal, frictional, structural, or cyclical.

- **Seasonal unemployment**

  Seasonal unemployment means you are not employed due to the seasonality of your occupation. Examples of professions that may fall under this category include lifeguards, gardeners, and ski instructors—if they live in seasonal climatic areas. For instance, a lifeguard who lives in a tropical area of the country year-round would not be seasonally unemployed! But what about a grammar school teacher, employed as a full-time employee by a school, who does not work during the months of July and August? Would this person be considered seasonally unemployed during those two summer months? The answer is no. Full-time (or "permanent") teachers, depending on the school, may opt to receive their yearly wages on a ten- or twelve-month basis. However, as they are receiving a "yearly" salary, they are not considered seasonally unemployed during the two summer months.

- **Frictional unemployment**

  Frictional unemployment means that, though you have the skill set needed in the workforce, you are in-between jobs. This generally short period of unemployment may be due to relocation. As an example, say your significant other receives a great career opportunity to move across the country—so you quit your job and start looking for a similar job at the new location. As another example, say you are working full-time at an accounting firm while going to school part-time. Upon graduating from your master's degree program, you decide to stop working in order to devote your full attention to studying for the CPA exams. In both examples, from the point you quit your job and until you are rehired by a new company, you are considered frictionally unemployed.

- **Structural unemployment**

  Structural unemployment means you are not employed because there is a mismatch between the skills you possess, and the skills required in the workplace. As an example, say you have been a bookkeeper for 20 years—but your company has finally decided to computerize its bookkeeping operations. As you are not computer-savvy, your boss fires you. You try to find another bookkeeping job, but you find that most companies want you to be skilled in QuickBooks. As you do not possess this required computer skill, you would be considered structurally unemployed.

- **Cyclical unemployment**

  Cyclical unemployment means you are not employed due to an economic downturn in the business cycle (i.e., the economy is at the lower end of the business cycle curve). As an example, during the 2008 real estate market crash, many workers whose jobs were linked to the real estate industry became cyclically unemployed.

Let's return to our previous question: is a stay-at-home parent; a billionaire who chooses not to work; or a student who leaves his/her job to pursue a full-time education considered unemployed? The answer is no. Assuming you are "in the labor force" but you are not ready, willing, actively seeking and able to work, then you are not considered unemployed. In essence, you have "removed" yourself from the labor force!

MEASURING UNEMPLOYMENT:

The Bureau of Labor Statistics (BLS) produces the unemployment rate for the nation, broken down by occupation and geographical area.[64] Specifically, the "Local Area Unemployment Statistics program is a federal–state cooperative effort in which monthly estimates of total employment and unemployment are prepared for approximately 7,500 areas." (Local Area Unemployment Statistics, 2017).

---

[64] See Labor Force Statistics from the Current Population Survey, 2018.

Figure 1 shows the seasonally adjusted unemployment rate for the United States from January 2007 to May 2017. You can see that the unemployment rate is highest during periods of historical economic downturns and lowest during periods of historical economic upturns.

Figure 1. US seasonally-adjusted unemployment rate (in %, from January 2007-May 2017)

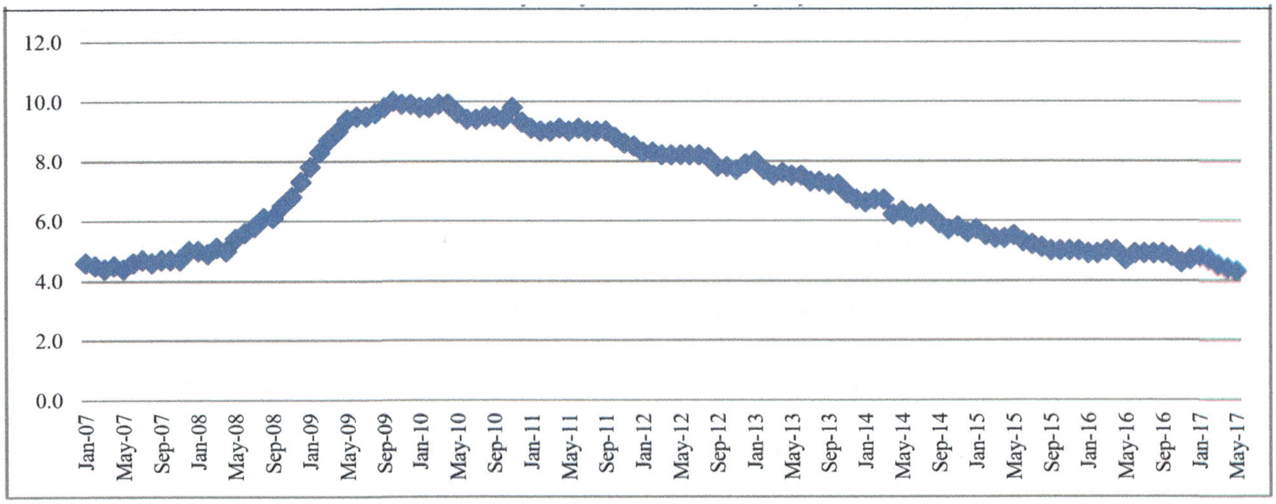

Source: Bureau of Labor Statistics, Current Population Survey, 2018.

The overall unemployment rate is calculated as the total number of people that are considered unemployed divided by the total number of people that are considered "in the labor force." Multiplying this ratio by 100 gives us the percentage of people that are unemployed.

The unemployment calculation is expressed as follows:

$$(\text{total unemployed} / \text{total labor force}) \times 100$$

Figure 2 shows a scenario which demonstrates, with numerical explanations, how the population is sectioned by those "in the labor force and those "not in the labor force". The scenario then calculates the different types of unemployment rates for this fictitious region of the country: total, frictional, structural, seasonal, and cyclical.

Figure 2. Unemployment rate calculation scenario

Let's say an upper northern region of the country has 10,000 total inhabitants, of which 15% are under the age of 16. Of the adults (over 16 years of age), 1,000 are retired, 500 are in the armed forces, 400 are in school, 350 are institutionalized, and 250 are disabled. We also know that 1,000 inhabitants are not currently employed. From this group, 200 are highly skilled and between jobs; 125 do not have the skills needed in this region; 100 are gardeners/landscapers; and 50 have decided to no longer look for work. Can we calculate the unemployment rate in this region?

The first thing we need to do is separate the inhabitants by category—those in the labor force and those not in the labor force.

Inhabitants Not in the Labor Force

Under 16 years of age (15% of 10,000)	1,500
Retirees	1,000
Armed forces	500
In school	400
Institutionalized	350
Disabled	250
Discouraged Workers	50
Total	4,050

Inhabitants in the Labor Force

10,000 (total) – 4,050 (not in the labor force)	5,950

Then we need to separate the inhabitants by employment category—those employed and those unemployed (also categorized by the type of unemployment)

Employed Population

5,950 (inhabitants in the labor force) – 1,000 (unemployed)	4,950

Unemployed Population

Structural: do not have the needed skills	125
Frictional: highly skilled and between jobs	200
Seasonal: gardeners/landscapers in cold region	100
Cyclical: not given, but can be calculated as,	
total unemployed – structural – frictional – seasonal	
1,000 – 125 – 200 – 100 =	575
Total Unemployed Population	1,000

Having calculated the population for each of the above categories, we can now calculate the unemployment rates for this upper northern region of the country.

The unemployment rate can be calculated as: (the total unemployed population divided by the total number of people in the labor force) multiplied by 100 (i.e., as it is expressed as a percentage).

Therefore, the expression = (1,000 / 5,950) × 100 = 16.81%

We can further break down the unemployment rate by type of unemployment.

2.10% [(125 / 5,950) × 100] of the population is structurally unemployed

3.36% [(200 / 5,950) × 100] is frictionally unemployed

1.68% [(100 / 5,950) × 100] is seasonally unemployed

9.66% [(575 / 5,950) × 100] is cyclically unemployed

Note, the process for calculating the unemployment rate(s) (as seen in fig. 2) can be applied to individual cities/states, grouping of states, categories of occupations, etc., as well as applied to the country as a whole.

The calculations of the unemployment rates in the above scenario begs the question, which of the four categories of unemployment is the government most concerned about? While all forms/categories of unemployment are of concern, seasonally unemployed individuals have the skills required to find jobs once their professions are "in season" again. (Also, please note that the BLS usually reports an unemployment rate that is already seasonally adjusted.) Frictionally unemployed individuals have the required skills, too, but are simply in between jobs, so their periods of unemployment are expected to be rather short.

However, structurally unemployed individuals pose a problem for society as they do not have the skills required by employers. These individuals will need to be retrained in the skills that are in demand in order to become gainfully employed. To assist these individuals, the government offers financial aid opportunities for unemployed people receiving unemployment benefits who want to go back to school (including trade and technical school) to earn a degree or learn a trade.[65] In addition, effective as of the Fall 2017 semester, all individuals making under $125,000 in gross earnings will qualify under the Excelsior Scholarship to attend a two- or four-year New York State college tuition-free.[66]

---

[65] You may visit the Federal Student Aid, 2018 website for further information on these assistance programs.

[66] Tuition-Free Degree Program: The Excelsior Scholarship, 2017.

Lastly, individuals that are cyclically unemployed are those that do not have jobs due to a downturn in the economy. Hopefully, when the economy rebounds, these individuals will become, once again, gainfully employed.

In the scenario in figure 2, while the region's overall unemployment rate is extremely high (16.81%), we also find that the primary cause of unemployment was due to the economy's downturn. Of the four categorizations of unemployment reported, the highest calculated percentage was in the cyclical unemployment category (9.66%).

NATURAL RATE OF UNEMPLOYMENT:

Somewhat synonymous with the term "natural rate of unemployment," the non-accelerating inflation rate of unemployment (NAIRU) is defined as "the rate of unemployment that exists when the labor market is in equilibrium (i.e., when inflation rates are neither rising nor falling)." In its simplest form, it is equal to the structural plus frictional rates of unemployment. Thus, furthering the unemployment scenario in figure 2, the NAIRU rate would equal 5.46%.
That is, 2.10% (structural) + 3.36% (frictional) = 5.46%.

Figure 3 shows the long-term natural rate of unemployment (beginning at 1970 and forecasted to 2020) and the civilian unemployment rate (from 1970 to 2018). The vertical shaded areas represent periods of recessions in the United States. As evidenced, while the long-term natural rate of unemployment hovers between 5 and 6% throughout, the civilian unemployment rate spikes immediately following periods of economic recessions.

Figure 3. Long-term natural & civilian rate of unemployment

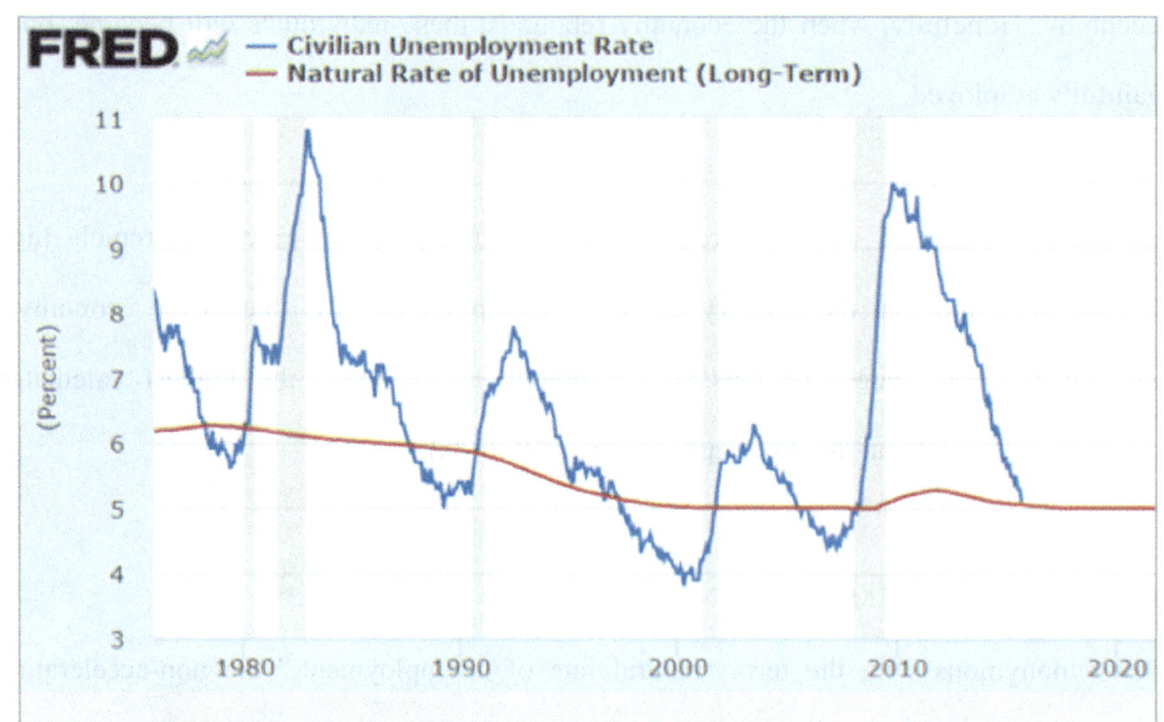

Source: FRED Economic Data St. Louis Fed, 2018.

UNDERSTANDING INFLATION:

At the peak of the business cycle, an economy faces inflation. Assume you are now ready to purchase a large plasma television; so, you search online to find "a good deal". However, you notice that the price has increased from when you last searched! Can you claim, "This is inflation"? No, an increase in one or a few products or services in the market is not inflation. Inflation may be defined as "a general increase in the price level of goods and services (or decrease in the value of money) in a nation."

So, how is inflation measured? In the US, three primary governmental agencies use proxies to measure inflation. The Department of Commerce calculates the producer price index (PPI); the Federal Reserve System calculates the industrial production index (IPI); and the Department of

Labor, calculates the consumer price index (CPI). The CPI program "produces monthly data on changes in the prices paid by urban consumers for a representative basket of goods and services."[67] The CPI is the most widely used proxy to measure inflation[68]. These rates are captured "cross-sectionally" (i.e., across the regions of the United States) and over time. Figure 4 shows the US non-seasonally adjusted average inflation rate from January 2007 to May 2017 measured from its growth in the base year 1982–84.

Figure 4. CPI of all urban consumers for all items (base years 1982-1984)

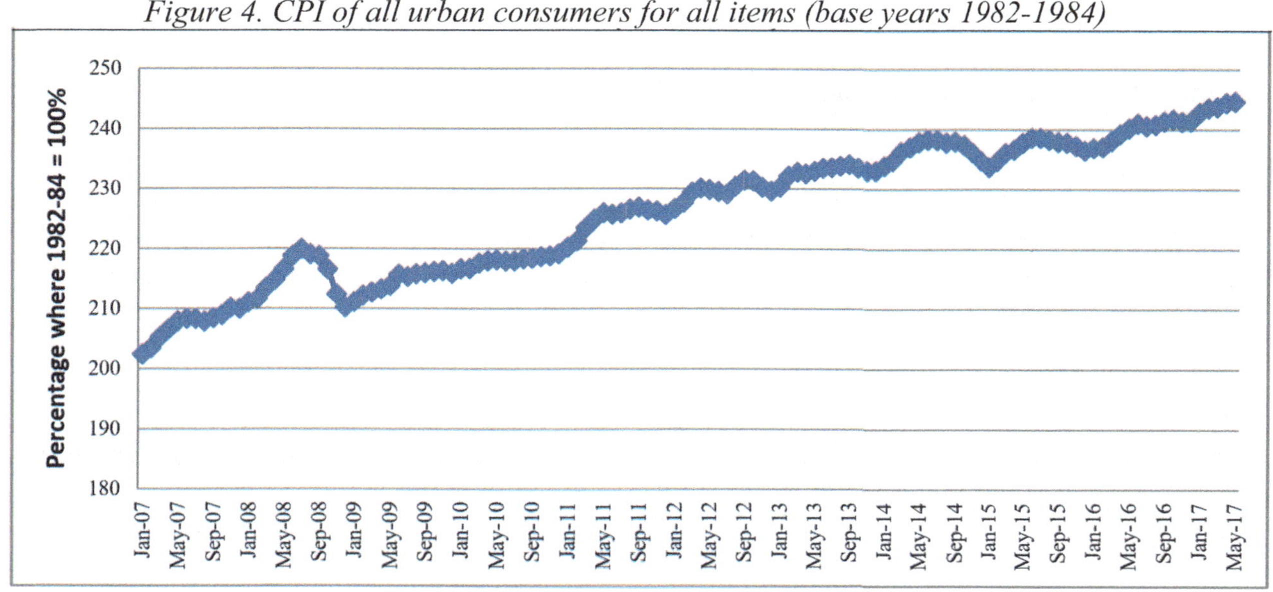

Source: Consumer Price Index, 2017.

We interpret January 2007 as follows: A CPI of approximately 200% means that, from the base years 1982–84 (where the CPI = 100%), the inflation rate doubled; or prices increased by 100%. Specifically, if an item cost $100 in the base years, that same item would cost $200 in January 2007—in other words, the buying power of $100 dropped to $50. BLS has a CPI inflation

---

[67] Consumer Price Index, 2017.

[68] In fact, if you google "inflation rate," most often, what is being shown is the CPI rate—even though the cite may not specifically state they are using the CPI index as the proxy for inflation!

calculator that you can use to quickly determine the buying power of an item between any two periods of time.[69]

Often-asked questions are, "is the CPI a surrogate for the cost of living"? "Can I use the CPI to measure the cost of living in another part of the country"? Remember, the CPI only tracks a basket of consumer goods over a period of time; it is used as one measure of inflation. However, also note that the CPI does not track all the costs (e.g., housing, utilities, health care, childcare, education, entertainment, groceries, and transportation) associated with living in any given area. Therefore, caution should be used when using the CPI as a measure of the cost of living.

Another often-posed question is "does everyone 'lose' when inflation is high?" The answer is no.

LOSERS & WINNERS DURING INFLATION:

There are "winners" and "losers" during inflationary times. Figure 5 lists people that benefit from periods of inflation and people that don't.

Figure 5. Who wins/loses during inflation?

Winners	**Losers**
° debtors/borrowers	° creditors
° younger/mid-income individuals	° wealthy retirees
° homeowners with fixed rate mortgages	° foreign investors
° indebted governments	° $-holding account balances

[69] See: CPI Inflation Calculator, 2018.

From figure 5, during inflationary times, the individuals/institutions considered "losers" have less dollar-holding or purchasing power due to a general increase in all prices. For example, the dollar value at which creditors receive repayments is worth less than the dollar value they loaned during the previous non-inflationary period. From figure 5, can you provide an example of why/how each of the individual/institution "loses" during inflationary periods?

In contrast, the "winners" refer to the fact that during inflationary times, the nominal dollar amount the indebted individuals/institutions have to repay in the future (i.e., equal to the amount of money they borrowed), has less real purchasing power at time of repayment. From figure 5, can you provide an example of why/how each of the individual/institution "win" during inflationary periods?

The following scenario (fig. 6), while fictitious, demonstrates (i.e., from a mathematical perspective) how individuals "win" during periods of inflation.

Figure 6. "Winners" during a period of inflation scenario

Furniture companies, to increase sales, at times offer payments on purchases over a period at zero percent interest. Taking advantage of this offer, you decide to buy a new bedroom at a price of $12,000 and make scheduled payments over the next year. Your monthly payment equals $1,000 per month. In the meantime, the economy is "heating up" and prices are beginning to rise. After seven months (i.e., seven payments), inflation begins to rise precipitously at an additional 1% each month So, while you continue to make your scheduled monthly payments at 0% interest ($1,000 per month), the inflation associated with your monthly payments rise as follows:

In month 8, the 1% increase of inflation on $1,000 = $10;

in month 9, the 2% increase of inflation on $1,000 = $20;

in month 10, the 3% increase of inflation on $1,000 = $30;

in month 11, the 4% increase of inflation on $1,000 = $40; and

in month 12, when you make your last payment,

the 5% increase of inflation on $1,000 = $50.

To summarize, during the first seven months, you paid a total of $7,000 (i.e., $1,000 × 7 months); and during the last five months, you paid a total of $5,000 (i.e., $1,000 × 5 months). However, inflation set in at an increasing 1% per month over the last five months of your payments. Adjusting for inflation, your furniture store should have received payment in the amount of $5,150 (i.e., the inflation-adjusted payments of $10 + $20 + $30 + $40 + $50 + the five $1,000 payments = $5,150). As you only paid a total of $5,000 during the last five months, the value (i.e., "purchasing power") of your payments decreased; you "made out"!

NOMINAL VS. REAL:

In comparing prices (e.g., wages, interest rates, etc.) you need to understand the difference between the concepts "nominal" and "real." The following example (fig. 7) will clarify this difference.

Figure 7. Wage inflation (real vs. nominal) scenario

> It's that time of year when your company announces next year's pay increases. As the company's profits have not increased as projected, it sends a letter to all employees stating that, unfortunately, the maximum percentage increase in pay will be 3%. As employees receive increases on a merit basis, individual percentage increases will be between 0% and 3%.
>
> With your next paycheck, you see an increase in pay and calculate its percentage. You received a 3% increase. You then find out one of your colleagues received a 2% increase and another received a 1.5% increase! Realizing this, you feel somewhat better about the raise you received.
>
> The next day, the inflation figures are published, and you read that the overall inflation rate for your area is 4%! Now are you happy about your raise? Did you in fact get a raise?

In the scenario in figure 7, the 3% increase is referred to as the "nominal" rate; this is the percentage rate stated before taking inflation into account. The inflation rate (4%) is higher than nominal rate (3%); therefore, the "real" rate is -1%. In effect, you received an inflation-adjusted decrease in pay of 1%; in other words, the purchasing power of your wages decreased by 1%.

Mathematically, in calculating the difference between nominal and real rates, the following formulas hold true:

nominal (rate) = real (interest rate) + inflation (rate)

real (rate) = nominal (rate) – inflation (rate)

DEFLATION:

In contrast to inflation, deflation may be defined as "a general decrease in the price level of goods and services (or increase in the value of money) in a nation." During deflationary periods, as the overall price level in the economy has decreased, consumers can buy more goods and services (than in non-deflationary periods) with the same amount of money.

But is deflation good for the economy? To answer this question, we need to note that a deflationary period is usually brought about by a deep and long-term decrease in the overall demand for goods and services. And the overall drop in prices signals an approaching recession. Declining wages (or no raise increases), unemployment, etc. generally follows.

How do we measure deflation, and is deflation synonymous with "disinflation"? The BLS describes deflation when the inflation rate is negative (i.e., < 0). Disinflation is characterized as a slowdown of the rate of inflation; however, the inflation rate is still positive. So, no, deflation is not equal to disinflation! To give some historical perspective, taken from the Monthly Labor Review's 2014[70] report, deflationary periods have occurred in the United States during the following periods:

[70] See, "One hundred years of price change: the Consumer Price Index and the American inflation experience", 2014.

Period	***Highest Deflation Rate***
August–September 1915	-0.7%
January 1921–February 1923	-15.8%
July–December 1924	-0.8%
July 1926–May 1929	-3.5%
July 1948–July 1949	-2.9%
August 1948–February 1950	-6.8%
July 2008–July 2009	-2.1%

From our earlier discussions in this chapter about the business cycle's polar-opposite negative effects on the economy, we need to ask, "How do we know we are heading toward a peak or a trough in the business cycle"? "At what stage of the business cycle are we in?" Or, "which stage of the business cycle did we just finish?" To help answer these questions, we turn to the three categories of economic indicators.

ECONOMIC INDICATORS:

The leading economic research organization, The Conference Board, has developed 21 economic indicators correlating with the business cycle.[71]

These variables are broken down into three categories: leading, coincident, and lagging.

- **Leading Indicators**

  There are ten variables that generally "lead" the direction of the business cycle. In other words, after these indicators trend upward/downward, the economy usually follows in

[71] U.S. Business Cycle Indicators, 2017.

the same upward/downward direction. Leading indicators are used to predict the upcoming direction of the business cycle. As an example, a business that is thinking about expanding its operations will feel more confident in making the decision if it expects the economy to be on the "uptick" (i.e., heading toward the peak of the business cycle).

- **Coincident Indicators**

  There are four variables that generally "coincide" with the direction of the business cycle. In other words, these indicators will cycle with the overall phases of the business cycle. Coincident indicators are used as a barometer to tell us where we currently are in the business cycle. As an example, while the business is hopeful that the economy will make a turn toward recovery, it will feel more confident if it can confirm that the economy is currently in the recovery phase of the business cycle.

- **Lagging Indicators**

  There are seven variables that generally "lag" behind the direction of the business cycle. In other words, after the business cycle trends upward/downward, these indicators later follow in the same upward/downward direction. Lagging indicators are used to "look backward" to ascertain that we have indeed completed a certain phase of the business cycle. As an example, a business may be skeptical if the economy is indeed in the recovery phase of the business cycle; it may ask, did we indeed "pass" the trough/depression phase of the business cycle? However, if it can confirm that one of the lagging indicators, say, the average duration of unemployment has decreased, it may feel more confident that the economy is on the "uptick".

Figure 8 lists the variables that fall under each of the categories of economic indicators. A full description of each of these variables (updated on February 6, 2012) can be found at Economic Indicators, 2018; see reference section for full citation.

Figure 8. Economic indicators

Leading Indicators	Average weekly hours, manufacturing Average weekly initial claims for unemployment Manufacturer's (Mfg) new orders, consumer goods & materials Institute of Supply Management (ISM) Index of new orders Mfg's new orders, nondefense spending on capital goods Building permits, new private housing units Stock prices, S&P 500 Leading credit index (comprising of 6 financial indicators) Interest rate spread (10-year Treasury bonds – fed funds rates) Average consumer expectations for business conditions index
Coincident Indicators	Employees on nonagricultural payrolls Personal income – transfer payments (in 1996 dollars) Industrial production index Mfg and trade sales (in 1996 dollars)
Lagging Indicators	Average duration of unemployment Inventories to sales ratio, mfg & trade (in 1996 dollars) Labor cost per unit of output in mfg (monthly change) Average prime rate charged by banks Commercial & industrial loans outstanding (in 1996 dollars) Consumer installment credit outstanding to personal income ratio Consumer price index for services (monthly charges)

Source: Data: Description of Components, 2017.

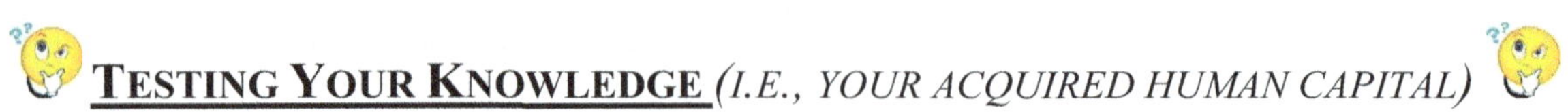

TESTING YOUR KNOWLEDGE *(I.E., YOUR ACQUIRED HUMAN CAPITAL)*

Determine whether the following questions are true or false. If false, can you explain why?

1. Is the CPI used as a measure of inflation?
2. Can some individuals or firms actually benefit from inflation?
3. Is another name commonly used for the natural rate of unemployment "the non-accelerating inflation rate of unemployment"?
4. Comparing situation A: nominal interest rate of 10% and inflation rate of 8% vs. situation B: nominal interest rate of 6% and inflation rate of 2%, would consumers borrow more in the first situation?
5. Referring to the business cycle, are economic variables that generally turn downward before a recession (and upward before a recovery) called "leading indicators"?

CHAPTER 10. MONEY & BANKING

THE FEDERAL RESERVE SYSTEM:

The administration of the United States' money and banking is controlled by the Federal Reserve System. The Federal Reserve Act of 1913 established the Federal Reserve as the central bank of the United States, providing a national banking system more responsive to the fluctuating financial needs of the country.

The United States and its territories are divided into twelve Federal Reserve districts. Each district contains a Federal Reserve bank that supervises all local banks. These twelve district banks are located in the cities of Boston, New York, Philadelphia, Cleveland, Richmond, Atlanta, Chicago, St. Louis, Minneapolis, Kansas City, Dallas, and San Francisco (in numerical district order). A geographical view of these central bank districts can be seen in figure 1.

Figure 1. Map of the US Federal Reserve Central Bank districts

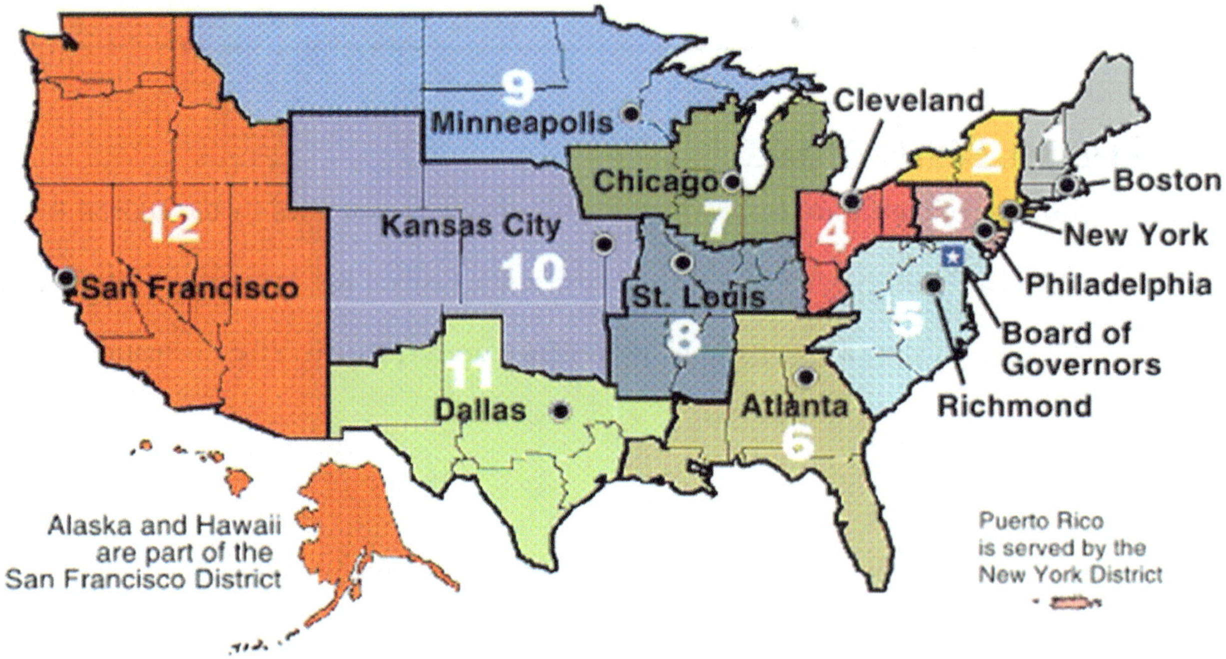

Source: US Map of Central Bank Districts, 2018.

These regional federal banks are responsible for meeting the physical currency needs of their local banks, providing cash and removing excess cash from the economy when needed. In addition, they remove currency out of circulation when it is deemed to be damaged, counterfeit, or just too old. The US Department of the Treasury's Bureau of Engraving and Printing (BEP)[72] sends them newly printed bills[73] and coins to replace the discarded notes and coins.

---

[72] The BEP is the agency that prints/mints currency for the United States. It has locations in Washington, DC, and Fort Worth, Texas.

[73] Note that the BEP prints twelve versions of the same bill—one for each of the federal reserve districts. As an example, say the Federal District of San Francisco requests additional $1 bills. The BEP will send $1 bills that contain the number "12" (the district number), the letter "L" (the 12th letter of the alphabet), and "Federal Reserve Bank of San Francisco" (the district's) name.

More specifically, the Federal Reserve System, performs five functions:[74]

1. It conducts monetary policy for the United States and controls the supply of money in circulation (M1, M2, M3).
2. It promotes stability of the financial system and minimizes “systemic” (i.e., undiversifiable or “the market”) risk by active monitoring and engagement.
3. It promotes the safety and soundness of financial institutions; monitors their impact; and regulates and enforces banking regulations.
4. It fosters the safety and efficiency of payment and settlement systems; and provides financial services to depository institutions, the US government, and foreign official institutions.
5. It promotes consumer protection as well as community development activities through the supervision, examination, research, analysis, and administration of consumer laws and regulations.

The Federal Reserve monitors the supply of money in circulation by classifying it into three categories.

<u>SUPPLY OF MONEY—M1, M2, M3</u>:

The three classifications of the supply of money is based on the assets’ liquidity (i.e., how easily the asset could be converted to cash).

M1 is considered the most liquid form of money; mathematically,

M1 = currency + traveler’s checks + checkable deposits.

[74] See: About the Fed, 2017.

M2 is considered quasi-liquid as it includes M1 and all intermediate liquid forms of money; mathematically,

M2 = M1 + savings deposits + money market deposits + small-denomination time deposits + money market mutual funds.

It is of note that the M2 money supply is roughly five times larger than the M1 money supply.

M3 is considered the least liquid form of money and represents the total amount of money in circulation; mathematically,

M3 = M2 + large-denomination time deposits + institution-only money market mutual funds.

Further defining the previously listed instruments,

- **cash**—Paper currency (i.e., notes) and coins.
- **traveler's checks**—Registered, non-interest-bearing notes (i.e., like checks) issued by financial institutions (e.g., "local banks", American Express, and Thomas Cook). A traveler's check carries the purchaser's signature and functions as cash. Unlike cash, traveler's checks can be replaced if lost or stolen.
- **checkable deposits accounts**—Non- or low-interest-bearing demand accounts where checks or drafts may be written. This includes negotiable order of withdrawal (or NOW) accounts on which an unlimited number of checks may be written. Usually, debit cards "linked" to these accounts make money readily available.
- **savings deposits accounts**—Low-interest-bearing demand accounts held at financial institutions.

- **money market deposits accounts**—Interest-bearing savings accounts, usually managed by banks or brokerage firms and insured by the federal government, with some characteristics of money market funds. A money market deposit account offers low rates of interest and checking privileges with limits.
- **small-denomination time deposits accounts**—Interest-bearing savings accounts or certificates of deposit (i.e., bank CDs) with deposits < $100,000. Bank CDs usually pay a fixed rate of interest until a given maturity date. Dependent upon the institution, the money in the fund either cannot be withdrawn prior to maturity or can be withdrawn with a penalty and/or prior notification.
- **money market mutual funds accounts**—Interest-bearing accounts where these mutual fund accounts invest only in money markets short-term (one day to one year) debt obligations, such as Treasury bills, certificates of deposit, and commercial paper. The primary goals of these funds are to preserve principal and to obtain modest dividend returns for investors.
- **large-denomination time deposits accounts**—Interest-bearing savings accounts or certificates of deposits (i.e., bank CDs) with deposits > $100,000. Bank CDs usually pay a fixed rate of interest until a given maturity date. Restrictions (e.g., maximum withdrawal percentages or penalties) on withdrawals prior to maturity will apply.

- **institution-only money market mutual funds accounts**—Money market mutual funds where eligible investors include "natural persons" + "non-natural persons," such as small businesses, large corporations, and pension plans.[75]

Figure 2 is a scenario demonstrating the calculation of M1, M2, and M3.

Figure 2. Calculation of money (expressed in billions of US dollars) scenario

Currency	$450
Savings deposits & money market deposit accounts	$1,400
Small-denomination time deposits	$1,000
Large-denomination time deposits	$5,000
Traveler's checks	$10
Money market mutual funds	$500
Institution-only money market mutual funds	$250
Checkable deposits	$490

Calculate M1, M2 and M3.

SOLUTION.

M1 = $950 billion = *450 (currency) + 10 (traveler's checks) + 490 (checkable deposits)*

M2 = $3.85 trillion = *950 (M1) + 1,400 (savings deposits & money market deposit accounts) + 1,000 (small-denomination time deposits) + 500 (money market mutual funds)*

M3 = $9.1 trillion = *3,850 (M2) + 5,000 (large-denomination time deposits) + 250 (institution-only money market mutual funds)*

[75] Of note, an institutional money market mutual fund is required to price and transact using a "floating" share price carried out to 4 decimal places (i.e., $1.0000). However, a non-institutional money market mutual fund sets its share price carried out to only 2 decimal places (i.e., $1.00). This difference, given the amount of the investment, can lead to a much higher rate of return for the institutional money market mutual fund accounts!

Quiz: Credit Cards & Money:

Credit cards are calculated in

a. M1
b. M2
c. M3
d. None of the above.

The answer to this quiz is d.

None of the above! Can you guess why?

Answer: Credit cards are not "money." Credit cards, issued by financial institutions or companies, are a form of "credit" (i.e., debt) given to credit-qualified individuals. A credit card allows the holder to pay for purchases at a later date (with interest if the payment is not made in full).

So, what is money and what are the functions of money? Furthermore, does the demand for money vary with the rate of interest? We will address these questions next.

The US dollar is the official issued legal tender of the United States, consisting of notes (whereby the physical paper note holds no intrinsic value)[76] and coins. The US dollar is considered the "money" of the United States.

Historical Forms of Money:

However, throughout history, many forms of money have existed. Some include gold and silver nuggets; rings, jewelry & precious metals; tobacco; ivory tusks; knives or large bronze blades

[76] "Zero intrinsic value" means the actual value of the physical notes (i.e., the paper) has no value. As an example, in the beginning of the 21st century, the nickel's intrinsic value was worth more than the nickel as a currency—because the value of the alloy (i.e., the nickel) was worth more than five cents! As a result, today's nickels are made up of a fraction of the alloy. This prevents the selling or melting of nickels to gain profits.

(China); cowrie shells (Indian Ocean); wheat (ancient Egypt); salt (East Africa in the Middle Ages), copper Katanga crosses (ancient Africa); squirrel pelts (Russia in the Middle Ages & modern Finland to some degree); and Lobi snakes (Ghana). While these forms of money were used as means of exchange, none of them fulfill all the four functions of money we now require.

Functions of Money:

Money serves four functions: medium of exchange, measure of value, store of value, and as standard of deferred payments.

- **Medium of Exchange**

  Throughout history, money has served as a medium of exchange. Buyers pay money to sellers in exchange for goods or services; sellers use money in exchange for other goods or services.

- **Unit/Measure of Value**

  Money measures and standardizes the value of goods and services; it assigns unit prices, or units of value.

  Money serving as a measure of value was very difficult under the barter system. Take the example of a doctor in a small town. What unit of value would the doctor "charge" to deliver a child or sew up a deep wound? Would the doctor accept the same remuneration for the same service delivered for all his/her patients? What if a patient was poor and could not afford the measure of value applied to services performed for wealthier patients (e.g., a chicken)? In this case, would alternative payment do (e.g., several eggs and some fruit)?

In addition, currency must be divisible as to make it possible to attach differing units of value to goods and services. This is why our paper currency comes in $1, $2, $5, $10, $20, $50, and $100 denominations while our coins come in 1¢, 5¢, 10¢, and 25¢ denominations. (With the other forms of money, as an example, can you imagine the difficulty in "dividing" up one gold bullion in exchange for a small-valued item, say a Big Mac?) Money, by performing its function as a common measure of value, has solved the standardization and divisibility difficulty and has facilitated trade.

- **Store of Value**

  Money must function as a store of value. This means that it can be stored/saved (e.g., at banks or in wallets) without the risk of being physically destroyed. This was not often true throughout history using other forms of money. (Can you imagine storing Lobi snakes or ivory tusks as forms of money?)

  The ability to store money, has facilitated the accumulation of money; thus, money has become the basis of promoting capital formation.

- **Standard of Deferred Payments**

  Deferring a payment means "paying for something at a later time (e.g., debt payments)." We defer payments by obtaining credit. Credit is paid in the form of money. Therefore, one of the other functions of money is that it can enable debtors (to make) and creditors (to give) and "track" deferred payments so that both parties do not stand to lose.

As an example, in some neighborhood stores, local customers may make daily purchases on credit, settling their accounts at the end of the week. This is referred to as "making deferred payments"—or, in more everyday language, "running up a tab"! This function of money allows the debtor (customer) to defer payments and allows both the debtor and creditor (store owner) to quantify the amounts of money spent and owed.

Why Hold Money-Three Motives:

Now that we have identified the functions of money, we ask a new question: why do people want to hold money in cash? We can identify three types of motives for people to hold money: transaction motives, precautionary motives, and asset motives.

- **Transaction Motives**

  The widespread use of credit & debit cards, online payment methods (e.g., PayPal), and apps (e.g., Venmo and Zelle (for Chase customers), has considerably reduced transaction incentives for holding money. However, many day-to-day transactions require people to hold money. Examples include small purchases (e.g., buying a hot dog from a hot dog stand); purchases in smaller rural areas or other parts of the world, where sellers only accept cash; donations/collections toward gifts; etc.

- **Precautionary Motives**

  People may hold money for precautionary or "emergency" purposes, such as to meet unexpected expenses, to "snatch up" bargains, or to pay for purchases when their credit/debit cards are declined/not accepted.

- **Asset Motive**

  The asset motive for holding money is sometimes referred to as the "speculative" or "investment" motive. People may want to hold on to money to take advantage of purchases which require cash! In portfolio management, your broker may "hold" some of your money in a cash account, so s/he can purchase the desired securities when the timing is "right"!

But does the amount of money people will hold—for transaction purposes, precautionary purposes, or asset motive purposes—change given their incomes? With all three motives for holding on to money, we find that (on average) a direct relationship exists: the higher the income, the higher the demand for money; and the lower the income, the lower the demand for money.

THE DEMAND FOR MONEY & INTEREST RATES:

Additionally, does the demand of money vary with the rate of interest? The answer is yes. An inverse relationship exists between interest rates and the holding of money. This is because if you hold on to money, or cash balances, you miss out on the opportunity to invest that money and earn a positive rate of interest. The loss of interest is the opportunity cost of holding cash in your hands. Therefore, the higher the interest rate, the less cash you will hold in hand; and the lower the interest rate, the more cash you will hold in hand. Figure 3 exhibits this inverse relationship.

Figure 3. Demand for Money

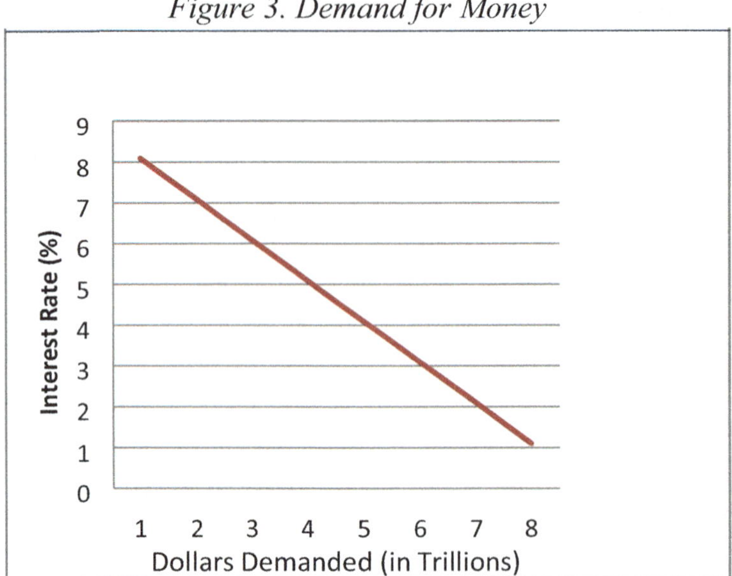

The demand for money (considering all three motives for holding it) will increase when the nominal level of output from the economy, such as GDP, increases (i.e., the curve in fig. 3 will shift to the right). The demand for money will decrease when the nominal level of output from the economy decreases (i.e., the curve in fig. 3 will shift to the left).

In sum, the demand for money increases when income levels increase and falls when interest rates increase; the reverse also holds true.

In this chapter, we discussed the functions of the Federal Reserve, the functions of money, and what determines the demand for money. In Chapter 11, we will continue with our discussion of the Federal Reserve, in relation to understanding the "tools" the Fed has to conduct monetary policy and how the equilibrium interest rate is established. In addition, a full discussion of fiscal policy, as well as the effects on the economy when both monetary and fiscal policies are employed will be explored.

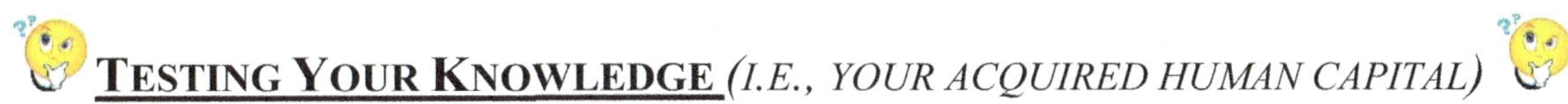

TESTING YOUR KNOWLEDGE *(I.E., YOUR ACQUIRED HUMAN CAPITAL)*

Determine whether the following statements/questions are true or false. If false, can you explain why?

1. The Federal Reserve System is comprised of 13 districts.
2. Does the Federal Reserve print the currency in circulation?
3. There is no opportunity cost in holding real money balances.
4. The central bank of the United States is the US Treasury.
5. Does M2 represent the total amount of money in circulation?

CHAPTER 11. MONETARY & FISCAL POLICY

MONETARY POLICY:

As stated in Chapter 10, monetary policy is administered by the Federal Reserve System (often referred to simply as "the Fed."[77] As a central bank, the Fed's three goals, specified by Congress, are to (1) ensure maximum employment, (2) stabilize prices, and (3) moderate long-term interest rates in the United States. It fulfills these goals by monitoring and controlling the supply of money in order to (1) manage the level of short-term interest rates, and (2) influence the availability and cost of credit in the US economy.[78]

THE THREE TOOLS OF MONETARY POLICY:

So, how does the Fed fulfill the stated goals? In order to conduct monetary policies, the Federal Reserve uses three "tools." It sets the required reserve ratio, sets the discount rate, and engages in open market operations. Let's look at these three tools in more detail.

1. Required reserve ratio (RRR)

The required reserve ratio is the portion, expressed as a percentage, of all depositors' dollar balances that a banking/depository institution must hold (i.e., always have on reserve against specified deposit liabilities) in cash. This portion of deposits (in dollars) cannot be used to engage in other interest-producing opportunities by the banking/depository institution. In other words, this money held on reserve cannot be used to make loans or investments.

---

[77] This is not to be confused with the federal government. The federal government's decision to stabilize the economy will be discussed under "Fiscal Policy."

[78] Board of Governors of the Federal Reserve System, 2017.

Banks use the following formula to calculate the dollar amount they must keep on reserve:

$$\text{required reserves} = \text{checkable deposits} \times \text{required reserve ratio}$$

or, $$RR \textit{ (in \$)} = CD \textit{ (in \$)} \times RRR \textit{ (as a \%)} \tag{1.1}$$

Where,

RR, expressed in dollars, is the currency amount that a bank must keep in cash and place on hold to provide clients with cash upon request. These reserves are usually kept in its vault or held at its district's central bank. The RR are a fraction of the institution's checkable deposits.[79]

CD, expressed in dollars, is the currency amount of all money deposited in any account in which checks/drafts may be written/withdrawn by a bank's clients. Checkable deposit accounts, therefore, include money markets accounts with checking privileges, NOW accounts, and checking accounts.

RRR, expressed as a percentage, is set by the Federal Reserve Board's Section D. It is the percentage of checkable deposits that a bank must hold on reserve.

At the end of each day, depository institutions must ask whether they have the amount of calculated RR on hand. One other simple calculation, that of excess reserves, helps in answering this question:

---

[79] Full information on reserve requirements can be found at the Federal Reserve's website; see Reserve Requirements, 2018.

$$\text{excess reserves} = \text{legal (total) reserves} - \text{required reserves}$$

or, $$\text{ER}\ \textit{(in \$)} = \text{LR}\ \textit{(in \$)} - \text{RR}\ \textit{(in \$)} \qquad [1.2]$$

Where,

ER, expressed in dollars, is the difference between the total amount of currency a bank has on hand and the total amount of currency it is required to have on hand [calculated in equation (1.1)].

LR, expressed in dollars, is the total amount of currency a bank has in cash/ currency at any point in time.

RR, expressed in dollars, is the currency amount calculated in equation (1.1).

Therefore, if the legal reserves are greater than the required reserves, the excess reserves are positive. In other words, the depository financial institution is holding on to more cash than it needs (as required by the Federal Reserve). On the other hand, if the legal reserves are less than the required reserves, the excess reserves are negative. In other words, the depository financial institution is holding on to less cash than it needs (as required by the Federal Reserve).

To better understand the calculations involved in banking reserves, see figure 1.

Figure 1. Banking reserves scenario calculations

A bank has \$500 million in total assets, which are composed of legal reserves, loans, and securities. Its only liabilities are \$500 million in checkable deposits. If the bank has \$60 million in excess reserves and \$80 million in total legal reserves, what are its required reserves? What is the required reserve ratio?

We will utilize equation (1.1), RR = CD × RRR, and equation (1.2), ER = LR – RR, to answer these two questions. In dissecting the scenario, let's add the appropriate acronyms to each of the given facts: "\$500 million in checkable deposits" (so, CD = \$500M); "\$60 million in excess reserves" (so, ER = \$60M); and "\$80 million in total legal reserves" (so, LR = \$80M). Let's start plugging these numbers into the two equations:

Equation 1.1: RR = CD × RRR; so, RR = \$500M × RRR

Equation 1.2: ER = LR – RR; so, \$60M = \$80M – RR

In looking at equation (1.1), we see that we have two unknown values: RR and RRR.

But, in equation (1.2), we can start solving for RR.

Algebraically, if ER = LR – RR, then

RR = LR – ER; so,

RR = \$80M – \$60M = \$20M.

The required reserves equal \$20 million.

We can now plug RR (\$20M) into equation (1.1): \$20M = \$500M × RRR.

Algebraically, if RR = CD × RRR, then

RRR = RR/CD; so,

RRR = \$20M / \$500M = 0.04.

Expressed as a percent, the required reserve ratio = 4%.

Can excess reserves be positive, and is that situation optimal? The answers are yes and no, respectively. While a bank can certainly have positive excess reserves, it is not an optimal solution as that "extra" money on hand does not earn any interest.

On the other hand, can a bank have negative excess reserves, and is that situation optimal? The answers are yes and maybe, respectively. Sure, a bank could make too many loans and find itself lacking the required liquid cash on hand. But can it simply ignore this situation? The answer is no; for the bank to stay in operation, it must cure its currency deficiency. In order to cure the deficiency, the bank will be forced to borrow money. As an example, if the bank's ER equals -$3.4 million, it must borrow $3.4 million. Therefore, the answer to the second question will depend upon the magnitude of two interest rates: (1) the interest rate on the present value of the interest income received from the source of the negative excess reserves *vs.* (2) the interest rate associated with the cost of borrowing to cover the negative excess reserves. If the interest rate earned in (1) > interest rate they must pay in (2), then the banking institution still benefits from running negative excess reserves. On the other hand, if the interest rate earned in (1) < interest rate they must pay in (2), then the banking institution is losing money and thus it is not optimal for them to be running negative excess reserves.

So, what is the cost of borrowing to cover the negative excess reserves, and where do banks obtain those funds? The short answer is, most of the time, banks borrow from banks that have positive excess reserves. But how do they know which banks have positive excess reserves or what interest rates these banks will charge them to borrow the money? To answer these questions, we turn to the federal funds market.

The Fed Funds Market:

The federal funds market is a private financial market where depository institutions participate in the lending and borrowing of reserves. These are unsecured loan contracts set for very short periods of time—generally from a few hours to two days.

If banks have positive excess reserves, they want to lend that money to earn positive interest; if they have negative excess reserves, they need to borrow that money at a particular interest rate. The interest rate that banks charge other banks to meet minimum reserve requirements is called the federal funds rate, or the "fed funds rate" for short. The interest rate that a borrowing bank pays to a lending bank is negotiated between the two banks, and the weighted average of this rate across all such transactions is called the federal funds effective rate. (We will discuss how the Federal Reserve influences this rate in our discussion of open market operations—the third "tool" of monetary policy.)

The graph in figure 2 shows the daily effective federal funds rate from July 5, 2005, to July 7, 2017. We can see this rate drop precipitately during the financial crisis of 2008. It is not until December 17, 2015, that we see the rate beginning to rise again.

Figure 2: Effective fed funds rate from July 5, 2005, to July 7, 2017

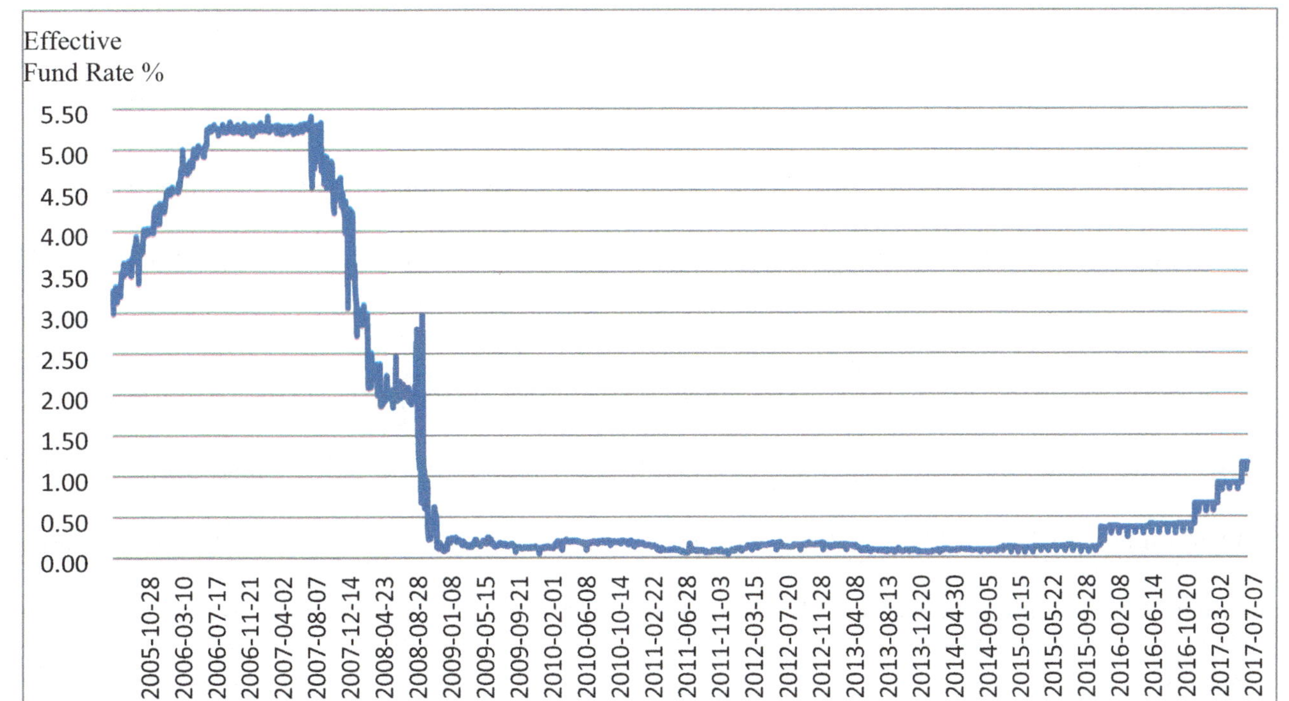

Source: Fed Funds Rate, 2018.

2. Discount Rate (DR)

The discount rate is another direct tool that the Federal Reserve uses to control the supply of money. Unlike the fed funds rate, which is influenced by the Fed, the discount rate is set directly by the Fed. It is symbolically used to indicate the direction of the change in interest rate policy the Fed wants to pursue for the economy. Specifically, the DR is the interest rate at which banks borrow from the Fed's discount window[80] to satisfy their negative excess reserves. Operationally, banks no longer physically send one of their representatives to the discount window. When a bank needs cash, it may request the funds from its local Federal Reserve. The Federal Reserve electronically deposits the requested funds into the bank's account and charges the appropriate

---

[80] The term originated when a bank sent one of its employees to a reserve bank teller window when it needed to borrow money. Today, the discount window allows eligible institutions to borrow money from the central bank, (usually on a short-term basis), to meet temporary shortages of liquidity.

interest rate (see fig. 3). Once the bank has excess cash on hand, it returns the funds to the Federal Reserve, settling the account(s).

While borrowing from the Fed may seem like an alternative method of financing negative excess reserves, banks are reluctant to borrow at the discount window for a few reasons. First, the Fed's discount officers monitor bank requests on a regular basis. Second, the securities market closely track the volume of the discount window's lending. In fact (beginning on July 21, 2010) the Fed now publicly discloses, after a two-day delay, full details about the borrowing institution: its name, the amount of its loan, and the interest rate. Third, unlike borrowing in the Fed funds market, loans made at the discount window must be secured by collateral with value equal to or greater than the amount of the loan. As a result, there is a relatively small amount of borrowing at the discount window.

Figure 3 presents the Federal Reserve's two discount window rates (primary and secondary) from the selected date of January 9, 2003, to June 15, 2017. The primary credit rate is extended to generally "sound" depository institutions on a very short-term (often overnight) basis. The secondary credit rate (also extended on a very short-term basis) is available to depository institutions that are not eligible for primary credit, ergo the higher rate![81]

[81] A full description of the discount window's lending programs can be found at: About the Fed, 2018; full citation found in the Reference Section.

Figure 3. Federal Reserve's discount window rates

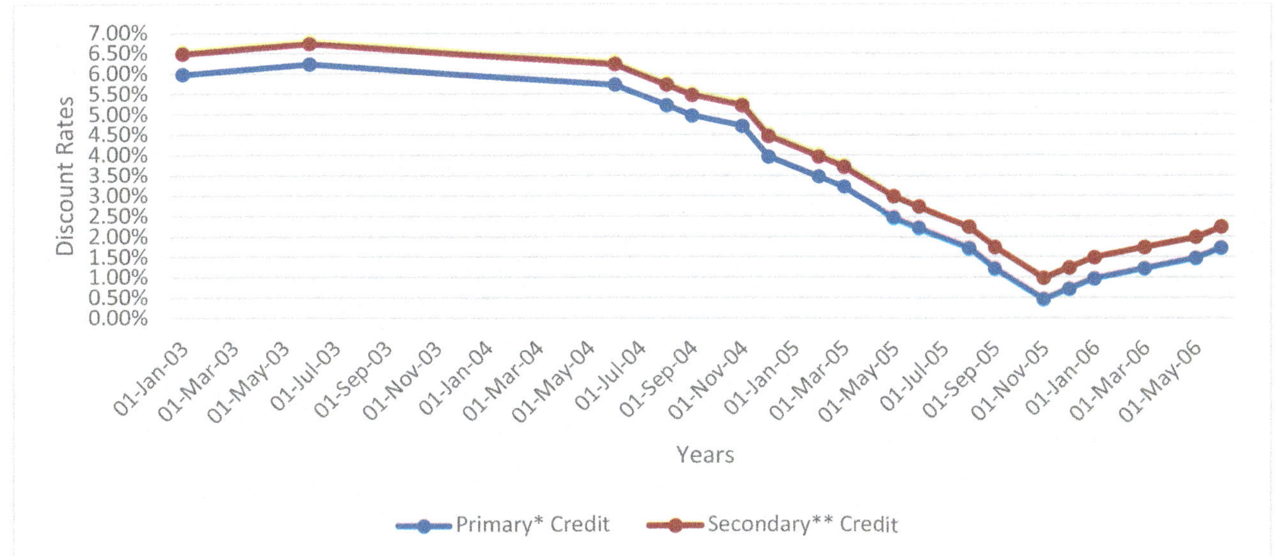

Source: Discount Window, 2018.

Compare figures 2 and 3. During the same time periods, the discount window rates (fig. 3) are higher overall than the fed funds rate (fig. 2). See figure 4 for a comparison of these rates for selected time periods. Thus, during these periods, it will cost a bank more money to borrow from the discount window than to borrow in the fed funds market. This is yet another reason why depository institutions are reluctant to borrow money from the discount window!

Figure 4. Effective fed funds rate vs. *discount window rates (primary & secondary)*

The Prime Rate:

Before discussing the third tool of monetary policy, one other interest rate deserves a mention. The prime rate is the interest rate that financial institutions charge on loans made to their best customers. This rate can vary by institution but follows, at a higher level, in the same general direction as the fed funds rate (and, to some degree, the discount rates). Many loans that banks make are based upon the prime rate. These include personal loans, car loans, mortgage loans, commercial loans, and credit cards. So, if you can meet the following combined qualifications (all indicating a very low risk of default), then the bank may give you a loan "at prime" (i.e., at the prime rate):

- you have excellent credit;
- you have sufficient income to cover the loan;
- the loan is secured (i.e., backed up by a security, such as a car or a house);
- and you are a long-standing customer of the bank.

Now, assume you have excellent credit, your income is high enough, and you are a long-standing good customer of the bank—but the loan you are seeking is unsecured (e.g., a personal loan to help pay off school loans). As there is now a higher risk of default, the bank may charge you "prime plus one." At a prime rate of 5%, this means that the bank will charge you 5% plus an extra 1% (6% total) for this unsecured loan.

Generally, the higher the risk of default, the higher the percentage the financial institutions will add to the prime rate.

3. Open Market Operations (OMO)

The third tool of monetary policy is the buying and selling of Treasury securities in the open market.[82] This is by far the tool used most often by the Fed to control the supply of money in circulation. If you recall from our discussion of the business cycle, if the economy is in a recession and possibly reaching the downward trough cycle, the Fed may want to stimulate spending to avoid high levels of unemployment. In this case, it can enter the open market and "buy" securities. It buys these Treasury securities, held by the investing public, through a competitive bidding process—not through a direct purchase from the US Treasury. By purchasing securities, the Fed puts "money" into the hands of the investing public.

Conversely, if the economy is "overheating" (i.e., reaching the prosperity peak of the business cycle), the Fed may want to slow the economy down to avoid high levels of inflation. In this case,

[82] Please note that the primary responsibility of conducting monetary policy rests with the Federal Open Market Committee of the Federal Reserve.

it can enter the open market and "sell" its previously purchased securities.[83] By offering securities for purchase in the market, the Fed reduces the "money" in circulation. The "reduction" is due to the fact that investors are buying the Treasury securities and not putting that money into the goods and services markets.

In summary, by employing the three monetary policy tools, the Fed can control the supply of money in circulation.

To relate monetary policy to the business cycle, again, if the economy is nearing the peak of the business cycle and inflationary pressures are feared, the Fed will employ what is referred to as a "contractionary monetary policy". The decrease in the supply of money in circulation may be accomplished by a reduction in reserve requirements, a reduction in discount rates, and/or the selling of Treasury securities in the open market. Notably, contractionary monetary policy may result in a rise in interest rates. Unfortunately, rising interest rates will spur an increase in the flow of foreign capital in the financial markets: As US interest rates rise, foreign investors—seeing an opportunity to receive higher rates of return on their investments—may engage in US financial markets. This surge in foreign capital may potentially increase spending (and the amount of money circulating) in the US economy. This effect is in direct contrast to what the Fed is looking to achieve: to contract the supply of money in circulation!

If, on the other hand, the economy is nearing the trough of the business cycle, and the pressure of high unemployment is feared, the Fed will employ what is referred to as an "expansionary monetary policy". The increase in the supply of money in circulation may be accomplished by an

[83] Please note that the Fed does not participate in competitive bidding at treasury auctions!

increase in reserve requirements, an increase in the discount rates, and/or the buying of Treasury securities in the open market. Notably, expansionary monetary policy may result in a decrease in interest rates.

Unfortunately, falling interest rates will spur a decrease in the flow of foreign and domestic capital in the financial markets: As US interest rates fall, foreign and domestic investors may start to see their US investments lose value (due to lower rates of return). This decrease in capital investments may potentially reduce spending (and the amount of money circulating) in the US economy. This effect is in direct contrast to what the Fed is looking to achieve: to expand the supply of money in circulation!

Figure 5 shows the direction of each of the Fed's policy tools used to contract or expand the economy. It also shows the tools' effects on interest rates and (opposing) capital flows.

Figure 5. Federal Reserve monetary policy actions

Contractionary Policy (↓ Money Supply)	***Expansionary Policy (↑ Money Supply)***
If fearing inflation:	*If fearing depression:*
» increase RRR	» decrease RRR
» increase DR	» decrease DR
» sell securities in OMO	» buy securities in OMO
Generally, this results in interest rates:	
» increasing	» decreasing
But this affects capital flows that moves the economy in the opposite intended direction:	
» increase capital inflows	» increase capital outflows

Up to now, we discussed many types of interest rates and how they affect the economy. But is there an "equilibrium" interest rate? And, if so, how it is set?

Supply of Money & the Equilibrium Rate of Interest:

Referring to Chapter 10 in the discussion of the relationship between the demand for money and the interest rate, we know that the demand for money curve is downward sloping. But what about the supply of money? Is this curve upward sloping?

Because the Federal Reserve through its monetary policy sets the supply of money in circulation, when graphed, the supply of money curve will be vertical. It does not vary with the rate of interest.

Therefore, the equilibrium interest rate arises at the point of intersection between the consumers' demand for money and the Federal Reserve's supply of money.

Figure 6 shows the demand for money curve and supply of money curve where the Federal Reserve has set a target for the supply of money (i.e., stock of money) to be $4 Trillion. Therefore, at the intersection of the demand and supply curves, we see that the economy's equilibrium rate of interest is 5%.

Figure 6. MS & MD: equilibrium interest rate

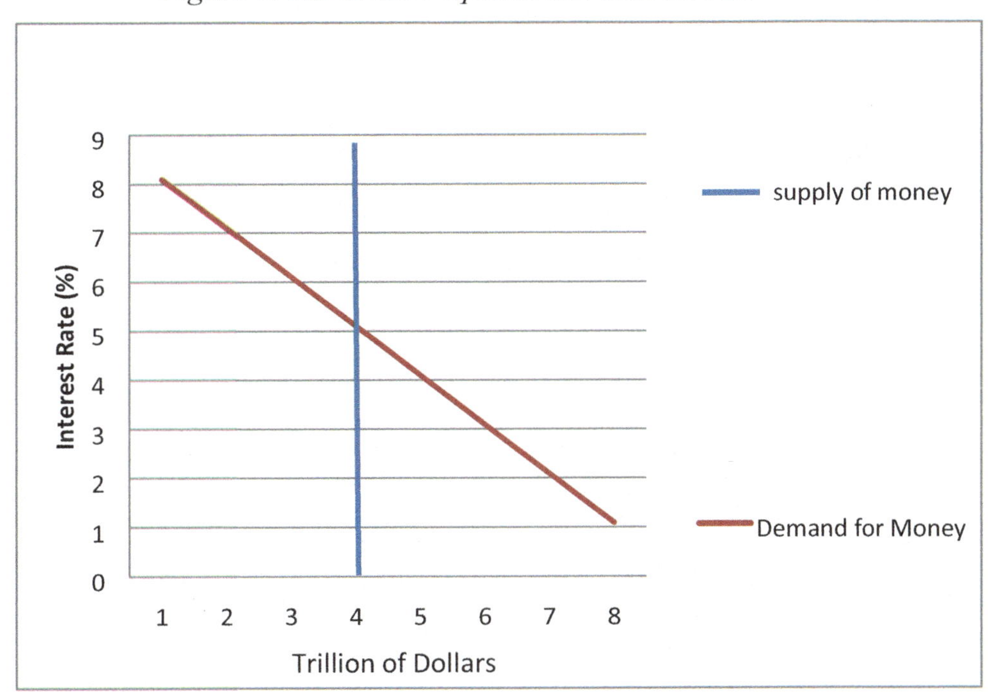

So, can the Fed set both an interest rate and a money supply target?

The answer is no!

Given the consumers' demand curve, the Fed can either:

1) set a money supply target. In this case, the equilibrium interest rate will be set where the supply curve intersects with the money demand curve (as seen in fig. 6); or,

2) set an interest rate target. In this case, the Fed must use the tools of monetary policy to increase/decrease the supply of money to intersect with the consumers' demand for money at their desired interest rate target (as seen in fig. 7).

Figure 7 shows that if the Fed wants to adopt an interest rate policy and achieve an equilibrium interest rate of 4%,[84] it will cause the supply of money in circulation to meet the consumers' demand for money at a rate of 4%. This means that the supply of money will need to increase from $4 trillion to $5 trillion.

Figure 7. MS & MD: shift in equilibrium interest rate

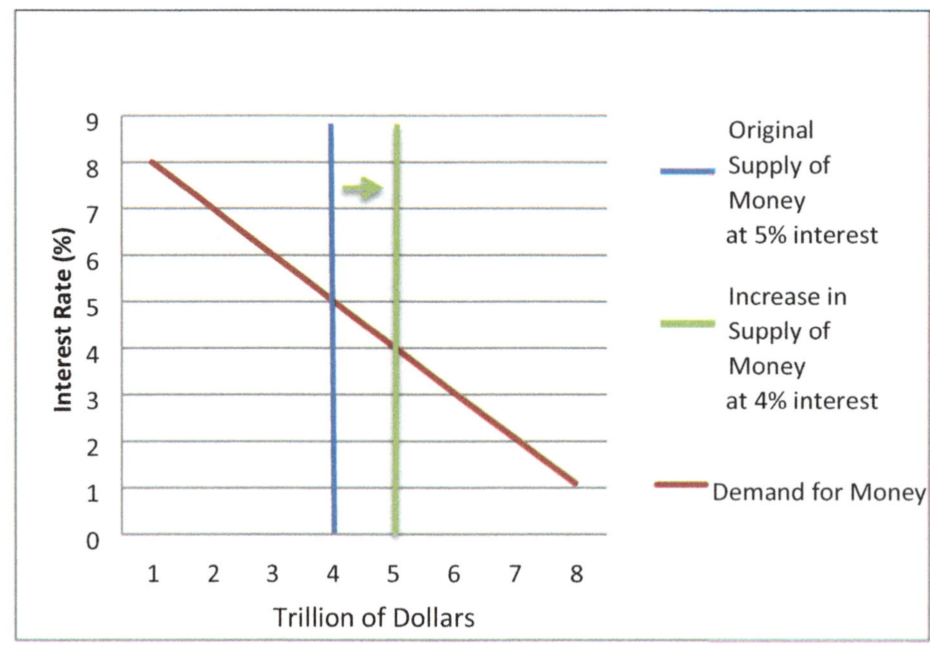

84 Again, the Fed can do this by utilizing the tools of monetary policy. In this case it can decrease RRR, and/or decrease DR, and/or buy securities.

In Chapter 7, we introduced the concept of "marginal propensity to consume" with the understanding that when one person spends an average 65% of his/her additional income, this spending multiplies by 2.8571.[85]

The same concept applies (i.e., that money multiplies as it passes from the hand of one consumer to another) when the Fed employs monetary policy, either expansionary or contractionary: it wants to know the multiplicative effect the money (that it removed or added) will have on the economy.[86] The simple money multiplier assists the Fed in determining this effect.

THE SIMPLE MONEY MULTIPLIER:

The simple money multiplier (m) measures how much the money supply increases in response to a change in the monetary base.

The simple money multiplier is measured as,

$$m = 1 / RRR,$$

Where, RRR = required reserve ratio

A Mathematical Example

If RRR = 10%, then m = 1 / 0.10 = 10.

Thus, for every $1 the Federal Reserve injects or contracts into the economy, the money supply will increase or decrease, respectively, by $10.

[85] See section "The Government Multiplier—Calculation & Interpretation" for a mathematical explanation of the simple government multiplier.

[86] This is so it does not increase or decrease the economy's money supply more than necessary. This avoids the overstimulation or under-stimulation of the economy!

Note, as of June 2, 2016, in the United States, the required and excess reserve requirements was 0.5%; therefore, the simple money multiplier at that time was 20 (i.e., 1 / .05). During this period when the Federal Reserve wanted to stimulate the economy, it knew that for every $1 injected into the economy, the money supply would, on average, increase by $20.

In sum, monetary policy directly affects interest rates while indirectly affecting stock prices (which are affected by interest rates), wealth, and currency exchange rates. Through these systems and by employing the three tools of monetary policy, the Fed influences consumer spending; business investment & production; and employment & inflation rates in the economy.

Lastly, please note that monetary policy decisions made by the Federal Reserve are independent of any policy decisions made by the federal government, even in terms of any borrowing and/or selling of Treasury securities. Monetary policy is therefore made independently of fiscal policy!

FISCAL POLICY

Fiscal policy is administered by the federal government. Its goal is to ensure economic growth while having a stable economy. In other words, the goal of the federal government (in terms of the overall economy) is to have an increasing per capita GDP rate over time while minimizing the ups and downs of the business cycle. (See fig. 8.)

Figure 8. Per capita GDP growth rate over time

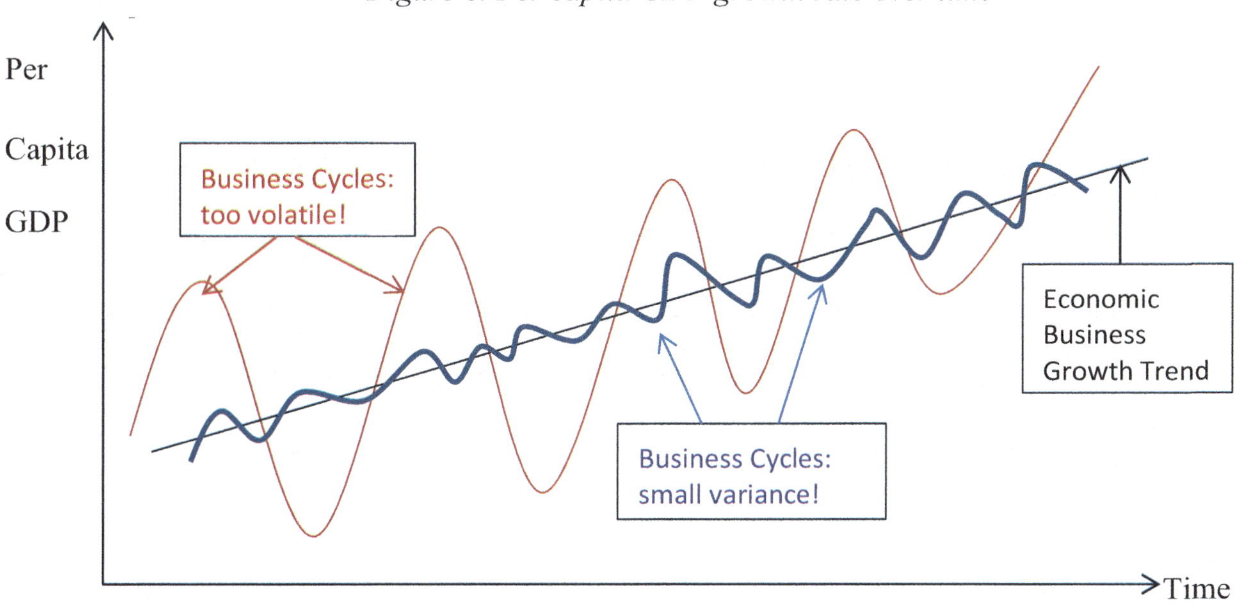

In contrast to the Federal Reserve, the federal government has only two tools at its disposal to stabilize the economy—government spending and taxation. The federal government can impact the economy by changing the level and type of taxes imposed; the extent and type of spending; and the degree and form of borrowing.

The government faces a balanced budget when government spending is equal to taxation, where government spending is considered capital outflow and taxation is considered capital inflow.

Considering political & administrative current challenges, the federal government can attempt to grow and stabilize the economy using these two fiscal policy tools.

If the economy is nearing the peak of the business cycle and inflation is feared; the Fed may adopt contractionary fiscal policy. This means that they can decrease spending and/or increase taxation exclusive of policies aimed at the foreign sector of the economy.[87] Employing contractionary fiscal policy results in a current budget surplus. This arises as the change in government spending (outflows of capital) is less than the incomes earned from taxation (the inflows of capital). In reviewing the expenditure approach to GDP (where GDP = C + I + G + NE), we can see that a decrease in G (government spending) directly decreases GDP. Furthermore, increasing taxation will potentially decrease C (consumption) and indirectly decrease I (investment spending). As a result, GDP may decrease by the amount of C + I + G.[88] Independent of the tools used, when employing contractionary fiscal policy, the economy will "slow down" its growth!

If the economy is nearing the trough/depression phase of the business cycle and unemployment is feared; the Fed will employ expansionary fiscal policy in an effort to stabilize the economy. Given the two tools of fiscal policy, this means that they can increase government spending and/or decrease taxation exclusive of policies aimed at the foreign sector of the economy.[89] However, this results in a current budget deficit. This arises as the change in government spending is greater than the incomes earned from taxation. Once again, in reviewing the expenditure approach to GDP, we can see that an increase in G (government spending) directly increases GDP. Furthermore, decreasing taxation in the consumer sector will potentially increase C (consumption), and decreasing taxation in the business sector will indirectly increase I (investment spending). Therefore, GDP may potentially increase by the amount of C + I + G; in other words, the economy will grow![90]

---

[87] See Chapter 7 for governmental policies aimed at the foreign sector of the economy.

[88] See Chapter 7 for equilibrium conditions in an open economy.

[89] See Chapter 7 for governmental policies aimed at the foreign sector of the economy.

[90] See Chapter 7 for equilibrium conditions in an open economy.

FINANCING THE GOVERNMENT'S DEFICIT:

But how does the federal government finance the current budget deficit when employing expansionary fiscal policy?

Should the federal government have a surplus in its current budget, it can certainly use that surplus to finance the deficit. But if the federal government does not have sufficient funds in its budget to finance the deficit, it can increase taxes or borrow the money from the public (i.e., enter the financial market) with the issuance of Treasury securities.

If the federal government raises taxes to finance its budget deficit, the effect may be in direct contrast to the goal of stimulating the economy. As such, the government must closely evaluate the level and types of taxes[91] it imposes to finance its budget deficit. If the federal government increases taxes in the private sector (e.g., higher income taxes), it will potentially reduce savings (thus having less money available to fund investment spending) and reduce discretionary income (thus causing consumption spending to decrease). If the federal government increases taxes in the business sector (e.g., higher corporation taxes), it will cause investment spending to decrease. *Ceteris paribus*, higher government spending financed by higher domestic taxes should not increase GDP as a rise in G (government spending) may be offset by a fall in C (consumer spending) and a possible fall in I (investment spending)—contrary effects when trying to stimulate an economy!

[91] It must carefully evaluate the level and types of taxes in relation to which industry to tax, which product(s)/services(s) given their demand/income elasticities, etc.)

If the federal government borrows the money to finance its current budget deficit, it can sell Treasury securities at auctions.[92] In this case, the Treasury determines the types and amounts of Treasury securities sold at auction with the goal of achieving the lowest financing costs over the borrowing period. On the other hand, the Federal Reserve does not participate in competitive bidding at Treasury auctions. But, similar to the Federal Reserve's autonomy of monetary policy decisions, the Treasury's debt management decisions are also not influenced by the Federal Reserve's purchases of Treasury securities in the secondary markets. Should the government finance its debt via the selling of Treasury securities, the "crowding-out effect" may occur. This negative effect is discussed in the subsequent section.

In sum, figure 9 shows the direction of each federal government tool employed to contract/expand the economy and its effect on the budget.

Figure 9. Federal government's fiscal policy (FP) actions

Contractionary FP	Expansionary FP
If fearing inflation:	*If fearing depression:*
» decrease G	» increase G
» increase T	» decrease T
Policy effect on federal government's budget:	
↑ budget: surplus	↓ budget: deficit

[92] The predetermined quarterly schedule of auction dates is published and made known to all.

GOVERNMENT'S CHALLENGES:

In employing contractionary or expansionary fiscal policies, the federal government is faced with three challenges:

1. **Time Lags**—Three phases: recognition, decision and effect

Irrespective of whether the federal government will employ contractionary or expansionary fiscal policies, it will be faced with time lags. The recognition phase is the amount of time it takes to recognize there is a problem in the economy's growth or stability that needs to be addressed via fiscal policies. The decision phase is the amount of time it takes to research and project what type and level of policy tool(s) will be used. The effect phase is the time it will take to see the effect the policies have on the economy and make adjustments if necessary.

2. **Crowding Out Effect**

The crowding out effect is a phenomenon that may occur[93] when the government enters the financial market to sell Treasury securities. Generally, the buyers of these government bonds are private individuals, pension funds, or investment trusts. Therefore, the crowding out effect occurs when the federal government is attempting to expand the economy or needs funding for other large expenditures, such as national defense.

When the federal government sells securities, it causes a decrease in investment interest spending and consumption. This is because investors and consumers (a) are buying the government's securities and therefore "crowding out" private sector investments (i.e., not buying securities from other corporations); (b) have less money to invest in private sector projects; and/or (c) are not spending money in the goods and services market.

---

[93] I use the word "may occur" as Keynesian economics argues that the crowding out effect will not occur during a recession in a liquidity trap since the government is merely spending unused resources.

3. **"Counter" effect on interest rate** when employing expansionary policy with a current budget deficit. When the government needs to fund its expenditures, as in the case of expansionary fiscal policy, it can (as stated previously) secure those funds by entering in the financial market to sell Treasury securities. However, in addition to the possible crowding out effect, the government may have to offer higher rates of interest on its government bonds in order to attract investors. These higher interest rates on bonds may push interest rates up on other securities and are likely to discourage private sector investing and spending.

Therefore, if the federal government wants to utilize the government spending tool to lead the economy out of a depression/recession, and if it finances this expenditure through the sale of Treasury securities, it runs the risk of increasing the economy's interest rates. Naturally, this is not the desired direction of interest rates during a recession!

But will interest rates always rise when the federal government sells Treasury securities? History tells us that during a recession, when the population is primarily risk averse (i.e., scared to invest in unsecured instruments), investors will use their savings to invest in government bonds. If there is a strong demand to hold bonds, then the federal government need not entice investors with higher rates of interest![94] In addition, when the private sector of the economy has idle or unused financial resources, businesses may be willing to absorb the debt of the government (i.e., buy Treasury securities). So, once again, the federal government need not offer investors higher rates of interest to entice them to purchase its bonds.

---

[94] This was evidenced during the United Kingdom's 2009–2013 recession.

In sum, barring any imminent danger to the economy (calling for immediate action to be taken), the time lag challenge will remain. However, the crowding out effect and the increase in interest rates effect may not always occur. These two effects are more likely to occur when the economy is growing and close to full capacity.

But how much money will the government have to infuse into the system or extract from the economy to achieve its desired effect? Similar in principal to the simple money multiplier, the government may turn to the simple spending government multiplier.

THE GOVERNMENT MULTIPLIER—CALCULATION & INTERPRETATION:

For policy purposes, how does the government measure the economy's spending multiplier?

The formula for the government's simple spending multiplier (g) is

$$g = 1 / MPS$$

$$or, \quad g = 1 / (1 - MPC)$$

As an example, as fully discussed in Chapter 7, assume that the marginal propensity to consume is 0.65. This means that for every $1 increase in disposable income, 65% of the additional disposable income in the economy will be consumed/spent. What the government wants to know is, if the government were to increase its expenditures, "what is the maximum amount that real GDP for the economy could change by"? As an example, what if the government injected money into the economy (i.e., say in terms of decreases in taxation and/or increases in direct government spending) by $1 billion? By how much will this $1 billion injection increase GDP?

To answer this question, we use the following formula for the government multiplier:

$$g = 1 / MPS$$

$$or, \quad g = 1 / (1 - MPC)$$

From this example, we know $MPC = 0.65$

But we know that $MPS = 1 - MPC$

Plugging the value of MPC $MPS = 1 - 0.65$

$MPS = 0.35$

Again, the government multiplier, $g = 1 / MPS$

Plugging the value of MPS $g = 1 / .35$

$g = \mathbf{2.8571}$

OR, equivalently, $g = 1 / (1 - MPC)$

$g = 1 / (1 - 0.65)$

$g = 1 / .35$

$g = \mathbf{2.8571}$

INTERPRETATION:

If the government infuses an additional \$1 billion into the economy, it will increase real GDP by 2.8571 times the initial infusion (i.e., by \$2,857,100). Similarly, if the government decreases its expenditures by \$1 billion, it will decrease real GDP by 2.8571 times the initial contractionary amount (i.e., by \$2,857,100).

Why does this multiplicative effect occur? As you know, money circulates. When you spend money, that money becomes income for that person. The receiver of your money will then spend a portion of that additional income, at which time it becomes income for yet another person. As this chain continues, it causes a "ripple" (i.e., multiplicative) effect. As an example, let's assume you receive a cash gift of \$100 and your MPC is 0.6. In other words, for every \$100 you receive in disposable income, you will spend $60. Let's also assume that 0.6 is the average MPC in the economy. Figure 10 calculates how much money this cash gift of $100 will create in the economy.

Figure 10. How an additional $100 creates $250 in additional spending

Person	**Additional Disposable Income (DI)**	**MPC**	**Additional Spending** (DI × MPC)
1	$100.00	.60	$60.00
2	$ 60.00	.60	$36.00
3	$ 36.00	.60	$21.60
4	$ 21.60	.60	$12.96
5	$ 12.96	.60	$ 7.78
6	$ 7.78	.60	$ 4.67
7	$ 4.67	.60	$ 2.80
8	$ 2.80	.60	$ 1.68
9	$ 1.68	.60	$ 1.01
10	$ 1.01	.60	$ 0.61
11	$ 0.61	.60	$ 0.37
12	$ 0.37	.60	$ 0.22
13	$ 0.22	.60	$ 0.13
14	$ 0.13	.60	$ 0.08
15	$ 0.08	.60	$ 0.05
16	$ 0.05	.60	$ 0.03
17	$ 0.03	.60	$ 0.02
18	$ 0.02	.60	$ 0.01
19	$ 0.01	.60	$ 0.01*
20	$ 0.01*	.60	$ 0.00
Sum:	$250.00		

* *This is due to rounding*

So, assuming an average MPC of 0.6, each additional $100 of disposable income (e.g., a cash gift of $100) creates a total additional spending of $250 in the economy. Another way we could calculate this is using the simple government multiplier formula:

$$g = 1 / (1 - MPC)$$

$$g = 1 / (1 - 0.60)$$

$$g = 1 / 0.4$$

$$g = 2.5$$

So, $\$100 \times 2.5 = \$250$

Therefore, the higher the MPC or the lower the MPS, the less money the government has to infuse into the economy to achieve a target of increased real GDP. Alternatively, the lower the MPC or the higher the MPS, the more money the government has to infuse into the economy to achieve a target of increased real GDP.

On the other hand, the higher the MPC or the lower the MPS, the less money the government has to extract from the economy to achieve a target of decreased real GDP. Alternatively, the lower the MPC or the higher the MPS, the more money the government has to extract from the economy to achieve a target of decreased real GDP.

For more detailed information about the federal government, you may want to visit the US Government Accountability Office (GAO).[95] The GAO provides "Congress, the heads of executive agencies, and the public with timely, fact-based, non-partisan information that can be used to improve government and save taxpayers billions of dollars." (GAO, 2017).

---

[95] Their URL is: http://www.gao.gov.

COMBINING MONETARY & FISCAL POLICIES:

While Monetary and Fiscal Policies are independent of one another, they are often used in tandem to ensure economic stability and promote growth in a country. Figure 11 is a table combining both the tools of fiscal and monetary policies that each of the agencies can use to meet these goals.

Figure 11. Effects of combining monetary & fiscal policies

	Contractionary Policies	***Expansionary Policies***
	If fearing inflation:	*If fearing unemployment:*
	» decrease G	» increase G
	» increase T	» decrease T
	» increase RRR	» decrease RRR
	» increase DR	» decrease DR
	» sell securities in OMO	» buy securities in OMO*
Results in:		
	» increased interest rate	» decreased interest rate**
	» increased flow of capital**	» decreased flow of capital**

*While the Fed may buy securities in OMO, the Federal government may sell securities if it faces a current budget deficit.

**A "counter" effect that will mitigate the intended policy effect.

You will notice that in employing the tools of monetary and fiscal policy, the desired effect is to decrease interest rates during recession/trough cycle and increase interest rates during prosperity cycles. However, "counter" effects may occur under each policy.

When employing monetary and fiscal tools to stimulate an economy, the overall goal is to reduce interest rates; however, the federal government's selling of Treasury securities may cause interest rates to rise. In addition, low interest rates may cause an outflow of foreign and domestic capital as investors seek higher rates of return for their investments in other countries. An outflow of capital will not help the economy to expand!

When employing monetary and fiscal tools to contract an economy, the overall goal is to increase interest rates; however, increased interest rates may attract foreign and higher domestic capital investments as investors seek higher rates of return. This inflow of capital will not help our economy to contract!

In conclusion, with many competing constituents and interests, and in this world of interconnectivity with spill-over and possibly conflicting effects, ensuring the growth and stability of a country is NOT an easy feat!

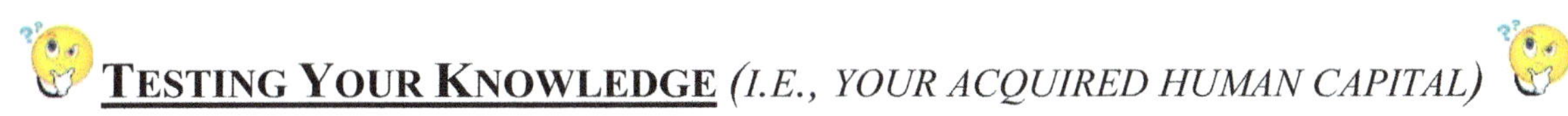

TESTING YOUR KNOWLEDGE *(I.E., YOUR ACQUIRED HUMAN CAPITAL)*

Determine whether the following statements are true or false. If false, can you explain why?

1. The interest rate at which banks borrow from the Fed's discount window to satisfy their negative excess reserves is called the "Fed funds rate."
2. When graphed, the supply of money curve, with interest rates measured along the y-axis, is upward sloping.
3. If $1000 was deposited into a bank and the reserve requirement was 0.10, $100 would be available for loans.
4. The Federal Reserve can set both an interest rate and a money supply target.
5. When the federal government wants to employ expansionary fiscal policies, it can increase taxation and/or increase government spending.

WORKS CITED

(2017, July 10). Retrieved from of the Federal Reserve System: https://www.federalreserve.gov/monetarypolicy.htm

(2017, July 27). Retrieved from Tuition-Free Degree Program: The Excelsior Scholarship: https://www.ny.gov/programs/tuition-free-degree-program-excelsior-scholarship

About the Fed. (2017, July 20). Retrieved from Board of Governors of the Federal Reserve System: https://www.federalreserve.gov/aboutthefed.htm

Alson, R. M., Kearl, J. R., & Vaughan, M. B. (1992). Is there a consensus among economists in the 1990's? *American Economic Review*, 203–209.

Big Mac Index. (2018, July 11). Retrieved from The Economist: https://www.economist.com/news/2018/07/11/the-big-mac-index

Budget of the United States Government. (2017, June 19). Retrieved from US Government Publishing Office: https://www.gpo.gov/fdsys/browse/collection.action?collectionCode=BUDGET&browsePath=Fiscal+Year+2016&isCollapsed=false&leafLevelBrowse=false&isDocumentResults=true&ycord=54

About the Fed. (2018). Retrieved from New York Federal Reserve: https://www.newyorkfed.org/aboutthefed/fedpoint/fed18.html

Big Mac Index. (2018, July 11). Retrieved from The Economist: https://www.economist.com/news/2018/07/11/the-big-mac-index

Capital Flight. (2018, October 9). Retrieved from Wikipedia: https://en.wikipedia.org/wiki/Capital_flight

Consumer Price Index. (2018). Retrieved from U.S. Department of Labor Bureau of Labor Statistics: https://data.bls.gov/cgi-bin/surveymost

CPI Inflation Calculator. (2018). Retrieved from U.S. Department of Labor Bureau of Labor Statistics: https://www.bls.gov/data/inflation_calculator.htm

Discount Window. (2018). Retrieved from New York Federal Reserve: https://www.newyorkfed.org/banking/discountwindow.html

Economic Indicators. (2018). Retrieved from The Conference Board: https://www.conference-board.org/data/bci/index.cfm?id=2160#BCI19

Exports of Good & Services. (2018). Retrieved from The World Bank Data: https://data.worldbank.org/indicator/NE.EXP.GNFS.ZS?name_desc=false&view=chart

Fed Fund Rate. (2018). Retrieved from New York Federal Reserve: https://apps.newyorkfed.org/markets/autorates/fed-funds-search-result-page

Federal Student Aid. (2018). Retrieved from U.S. Department of Education: http://studentaid.ed.gov/opportunity/

FRED Economic Data St. Louis Fed. (2018). *Economic Research*. Retrieved from Federal Reserve Bank of St. Louis: https://fred.stlouisfed.org

Labor Force Statistics from the Current Population Survey. (2018). Retrieved from United States Department of Labor: Bureau of Labor Statistics: http://www.bls.gov/cps/cps_htgm.htm

Lustig, N. (1995, June 1). *The Mexican Peso Crisis: The Foreseeable and the Surprise.* Retrieved from Brookings Report: https://www.brookings.edu/research/the-mexican-peso-crisis-the-foreseeable-and-the-surprise/

Marz, M. (2018, October 27). *Can I Get Into Trouble if My Employer Pays Me Under the Table?* Retrieved from The Nest:

https://woman.thenest.com/can-trouble-employer-pays-under-table-14625.html

One hundred years of price change: the Consumer Price Index and the American inflation experience. (2014, April). Retrieved from Monthly Labor Review. United States Department of Labor, Bureau of Labor Statistics: https://www.bls.gov/opub/mlr/2014/article/one-hundred-years-of-price-change-the-consumer-price-index-and-the-american-inflation-experience.htm

Prohibited and Restricted Items. (2018, October). Retrieved from U.S. Customs and Border Protection : https://www.cbp.gov/travel/us-citizens/know-before-you-go/prohibited-and-restricted-items

Reserve Requirements. (2018). Retrieved from Federal Reserve: Monetary Policy: https://www.federalreserve.gov/monetarypolicy/reservereq.htm

Rosenfeld, E. (2016, January 7). *Chinese yuan: Here's what's happening to the currency.* Retrieved from CNBC Currency News: https://www.cnbc.com/2016/01/07/chinese-yuan-heres-whats-happening-to-the-currency.html

Salama, A. (2015, June 31). *Market Mythbusting: The "Strong" Correlation between USD and US Stocks.* Retrieved from FX Street: https://www.fxstreet.com/analysis/indices-insider/2015/03/31/06

Shima, K. (2016). Market Structure and Investment . *International Journal of Finance & Accounting*, 30-35.

State Farm to stop insuring Florida. (2009, January 27). Retrieved from CNN Money: https://money.cnn.com/2009/01/27/news/companies/florida_insurance/

Statistic Brain Research Institute. (2018). *Black Friday Yearly Spending.*

U.S. Map of Central Bank Districts. (2018). Retrieved from Federal Reserve: https://www.federalreserve.gov/gifjpg/usmap3.gif

Wagner, J. (2012, July 4). *Interest Rates & the Forex Market.* Retrieved from Daily FX: Foreign Market News & Analysis: https://www.dailyfx.com/forex-education/intermediate/forex-articles/2012/07/04/Interest_Rates_and_the_FX_Market.html

Wei, L., & Vaishampayan, S. (2017, September 8). *Yuan's Surprise Strength Handcuffs China's Ability to Manage Economic Decline* . Retrieved from The Wall Street Journal Markets: https://www.wsj.com/articles/yuans-sharp-rise-muddles-chinas-growth-picture-1504776603

Chin, M. (2017, May 8). *LaVar Ball Gives Ridiculous Excuse for Why Baller Brand Sneakers Cost More Than Jordans.* Retrieved from Hypebeast: https://hypebeast.com/2017/5/lavar-ball-baller-brand-cost-more-than-jordans-excuse

Consumer Price Index. (2017, July 3). Retrieved from US Department of Labor Bureau of Labor Statistics: https://www.bls.gov/cpi/

CPI Inflation Calculator. (2018). Retrieved from US Department of Labor Bureau of Labor Statistics: https://www.bls.gov/data/inflation_calculator.htm

Data: Description of Components. (2017, July 5). Retrieved from The Conference Board: https://www.conference-board.org/data/bci/index.cfm?id=2160

Discount Window. (2018). Retrieved from Federal Reserve Bank of New York: https://www.newyorkfed.org/banking/discountwindow.html

Economic Indicators. (2018). Retrieved from The Conference Board: https://www.conference-board.org/data/bci/index.cfm?id=2160#BCI19

Exports of Goods & Services (% of GDP). (2018). Retrieved from The World Bank Data: https://data.worldbank.org/indicator/NE.EXP.GNFS.ZS?name_desc=false&view=chart

Fed Funds Rate. (2018). Retrieved from Federal Reserve Bank of New York: https://apps.newyorkfed.org/markets/autorates/fed%20funds

Federal Spending: Where Does the Money Go. (2017, July 26). Retrieved from National Priorities Project: https://www.nationalpriorities.org/budget-basics/federal-budget-101/spending/

Federal Student Aid. (2018). Retrieved from US Department of Education: https://studentaid.ed.gov/sa/

Frankel, J. (2017, June 28). *Carried Away: Everything You Always Wanted to Know about the Carry Trade, and Perhaps Much More.* Retrieved from: https://www.hks.harvard.edu/fs/jfrankel/CarryTradeMilkenInReview.pdf

FRED Economic Data St. Louis Fed. (2018). *Economic Research*. Retrieved from Federal Reserve Bank of St. Louis: https://fred.stlouisfed.org

GAO. (2017, July 17). Retrieved from US Government Accountability Office: http://www.gao.gov/resources/journalists/overview

Hot Dog Buns. (2017, June 5). Retrieved from Jet: https://jet.com/search?term=hot%20dog%20buns

Hot Dogs. (2017, June 5). Retrieved from Jet: https://jct.com/search?term=hot%20dogs

Households and NPISHs Final consumption expenditure (annual % growth). (2017, June 14). Retrieved from The World Bank: http://data.worldbank.org/indicator/NE.CON.PRVT.KD.ZG?year_high_desc=true

Households and NPISHs Final consumption expenditure per capita growth (annual %). (2017, June 14). Retrieved from The World Bank: http://data.worldbank.org/indicator/NE.CON.PRVT.PC.KD.ZG?name_desc=true

JEL Classification System / EconLit Subject Descriptors. (2017, July 18). Retrieved from American Economic Association: https://www.aeaweb.org/econlit/jelCodes.php

Labor Force Statistics from the Current Population Survey. (2018). Retrieved from US Department of Labor Bureau of Labor Statistics: http://www.bls.gov/cps/cps_htgm.htm

Local Area Unemployment Statistics. (2017, July 3). Retrieved from US Department of Labor Bureau of Labor Statistics: https://www.bls.gov/lau/lauov.htm

LaRocca, Richard, Frank DeSimone, Mary Lo Re, Ian Wise. (2017) Abstract: *"Currency Manipulations and Cultural Dimensions: A Perspective on the Evaluation of the Euro"*, Academy of Business Research, Fall 2017 Conference, Atlantic City, NJ Conference Proceedings; pg. 43.

Lo Re, Mary. (July 2011) *"Impact of the Global Financial Crisis on the EU and Euro Area vs. the USA"*. China-USA Business Review, David Publishing Company, IL, Vol. 10, No, 7, pgs. 532–538.

Lo Re, Mary & Cathyann Tully. (2011) *"European Union: Unification and Convergence"*. International Journal of Economics & Business Review, Inderscience Enterprises Ltd., Vol. 3, No. 3, pgs. 262–82. Also available on Econ Papers hosted by the Örebro University School of Business https://econpapers.repec.org/article/idsijecbr/v_3a3_3ay_3a2011_3ai_3a3_3ap_3a262-282.htm

Lustig, N. (1995, June 1). *The Mexican Peso Crisis: The Foreseeable and the Surprise.* Retrieved from Brookings Institution:

https://www.brookings.edu/research/the-mexican-peso-crisis-the-foreseeable-and-the-surprise/

Marz, M. (2018, October 27). *Can I Get Into Trouble if My Employer Pays Me Under the Table?* Retrieved from The Nest: https://woman.thenest.com/can-trouble-employer-pays-under-table-14625.html

Minimum Wage. (2017, June 9). Retrieved from New York State Department of Labor: https://labor.ny.gov/workerprotection/laborstandards/workprot/minwage.shtm

One hundred years of price change: the Consumer Price Index and the American inflation experience (2014, April). Retrieved from Monthly Labor Review. US Department of Labor Bureau of Labor Statistics: https://www.bls.gov/opub/mlr/2014/article/one-hundred-years-of-price-change-the-consumer-price-index-and-the-american-inflation-experience.htm

Prohibited and Restricted Items. (2018, October). Retrieved from US Customs and Border Protection: https://www.cbp.gov/travel/us-citizens/know-before-you-go/prohibited-and-restricted-items

Reserve Requirements. (2018). Retrieved from Board of Governors of the Federal Reserve System: Monetary Policy: https://www.federalreserve.gov/monetarypolicy/reservereq.htm

Rosenfeld, E. (2016, January 7). *Chinese yuan: Here's what's happening to the currency.* Retrieved from CNBC: https://www.cnbc.com/2016/01/07/chinese-yuan-heres-whats-happening-to-the-currency.html

Salama, A. (2015, June 31). *Market Mythbusting: The "Strong" Correlation between USD and US Stocks.* Retrieved from FXStreet: https://www.fxstreet.com/analysis/indices-insider/2015/03/31/06

Shima, K. (2016). Market Structure and Investment. *International Journal of Finance & Accounting*, 30–35.

State Farm to stop insuring Florida. (2009, January 27). Retrieved from CNN Money: https://money.cnn.com/2009/01/27/news/companies/florida_insurance/

Statistic Brain. (2016, August 3). *Black Friday Consumer Spending Statistics*. Retrieved from Statistic Brain Research Institute: http://www.statisticbrain.com/black-friday-yearly-spending/

Statistic Brain (2017, April 1). Shoe Size Averages. Retrieved from Statistic Brain Research Institute: http://www.statisticbrain.com/shoe-size-averages/

The Department of Homeland Security. (2017, June 19). *Basic Importing and Exporting.* Retrieved from US Customs and Border Protection: https://www.cbp.gov/trade/basic-import-export

US Business Cycle Indicators. (2017, July 5). Retrieved from The Conference Board: https://www.conference-board.org/data/bcicountry.cfm?cid=1

US Map of Central Bank Districts. (2018). Retrieved from Federal Reserve: https://www.federalreserve.gov/gifjpg/usmap3.gif

Video Games Market Research & Business Solutions. (2017, September 8). Retrieved from NPD Group: https://www.npd.com/wps/portal/npd/us/industry-expertise/video-games/

Minimum Wage Laws in the States. (2017, June 9). Retrieved from United States Department of Labor: https://www.dol.gov/whd/minwage/america.htm

Wagner, J. (2012, July 4). *Interest Rates & the FX Market.* Retrieved from DailyFX: https://www.dailyfx.com/forex-education/intermediate/forex-articles/2012/07/04/Interest_Rates_and_the_FX_Market.html

Wei, L., & Vaishampayan, S. (2017, September 8). *Yuan's Surprise Strength Handcuffs China's Ability to Manage Economic Decline.* Retrieved from The Wall Street Journal: https://www.wsj.com/articles/yuans-sharp-rise-muddles-chinas-growth-picture-1504776603

INDEX

Made in the USA
Coppell, TX
13 April 2025

48149458R00129